U.S. Energy R & D Policy

During the past few decades there has been an advance in the research and development of solving the issue of declining energy resources. Funding by the U.S. government into energy research has risen steeply. Because of the growing importance of research and development in this field of research, in 1973 Resources for the Future undertook a study of energy-associated study, including an investigation of how research on energy R & D itself could be carried out. This title, first published in 1974, assesses a wide range of ways in which economics could contribute to decisions on where and in what amounts government R & D money should be spent. The report also evaluates the research and development approach in relation to other public energy policies or management tools. The book will be of interest to students of environmental studies and economics.

U.S. Energy R & D Policy

The Role of Economics

John E. Tilton

RFF PRESS
RESOURCES FOR THE FUTURE

First published in 1974
by Resources for the Future, Inc.

This edition first published in 2015 by Routledge
2 Park Square, Milton Park, Abingdon, Oxon, OX14 4RN
and by Routledge
711 Third Avenue, New York, NY 10017

Routledge is an imprint of the Taylor & Francis Group, an informa business

© 1974 Resources for the Future, Inc.

Publisher's Note
The publisher has gone to great lengths to ensure the quality of this reprint but points out that some imperfections in the original copies may be apparent.

Disclaimer
The publisher has made every effort to trace copyright holders and welcomes correspondence from those they have been unable to contact.

A Library of Congress record exists under LC control number: 74021753

ISBN 13: 978-1-138-92991-3 (hbk)
ISBN 13: 978-1-315-68079-8 (ebk)

U.S. ENERGY R & D POLICY

The Role of Economics

John E. Tilton

A Resources for the Future Study
Supported by the National Science Foundation
Grant No. ATA 73-07742 A02

Resources for the Future, Inc.
Washington, D. C.

September 1974

RFF WORKING PAPER EN-4

This material has been published as received without the usual editing and type-
setting in order to speed its distribution.

Library of Congress Catalog Card Number 74-21753
ISBN 0-8018-1705-6

RFF Working Paper EN-4 $3.50

TABLE OF CONTENTS

PREFACE

The human instinct for seeking panaceas for complex problems has
operated during the past two years to advance research and development
as the remedy for the nation's energy problems. Funding by the federal
government in this area has risen steeply, and Congress and the Executive
appear to be engaged in competition to see who can aim highest in annual
expenditures.

While the amounts involved are still small compared with, say, defense
spending, two billion dollars of federal funds each year for the next five
years begins to be a sizable amount. Normally, such investments would
come under close scrutiny with regard to their likely benefits, but in
matters of research and development the public tends to assume that the
money is being appropriated for a worthy purpose. Also, it is very difficult to assess either the potential success of a project or the consequences of success.

Because of the growing importance of research and development in the
national budget, in 1973 Resources for the Future, with the support of the
National Science Foundation, undertook a study of energy-associated research
needs in the social sciences, including an investigation of how research on
energy R&D itself could be carried out. In the resulting work, Energy and
the Social Sciences--An Examination of Research Needs, the latter subject
is dealt with primarily in terms of the variables determining R&D activities
in the private sector, and a number of questions are raised on what kind of
research can and should be done.

An additional set of issues--the variables to be considered in public
decision making on R&D--were deemed of sufficient importance to prompt the
commissioning of a paper on the subject. John Tilton, Associate Professor

of Mineral Economics at The Pennsylvania State University, prepared this
paper describing and assessing a wide range of ways in which economics
could contribute to decisions on where and in what amounts government R&D
dollars should be spent. He also evaluated the research and development
approach in relation to other public energy policies or management tools.
To explore his views thoroughly, his paper and the issues raised in it
were subjected to review at an interdisciplinary seminar held in mid-April.
Professor Tilton's care in preparing the report was matched by his patience
in listening to critical remarks at the seminar. We owe him thanks for
both.

This report then contains the paper as well as the approaches suggested in the ensuing seminar. The reader will decide for himself how
large the contribution of economics is or can be, and to what extent the
political process is apt to sweep aside whatever economists, even if they
speak unanimously, have to say about costs and benefits from energy research
and development. In making that decision the reader will be helped by
Part II, which contains some statements made at the seminar that seem
particularly succinct or otherwise apt to throw light on the matter.

To some persons all this may seem an exercise in futility now that
the country is firmly embarked upon a large energy R&D program and the time
for thinking about how to fashion it is past. It is a respectable view,
but sometimes realism can be carried too far. No policy is ever final, and
"too late" is at times a ready excuse for refusing to rethink a difficult
problem. It is in that frame of mind that RFF offers this monograph. Those
who want to continue thinking about public decision making on energy R&D
may find it a useful aid in clarifying the elements of current and future
policies.

The financial assistance offered by NSF is gratefully acknowledged. Beyond that, the personal interest and enthusiasm of Paul Craig, who during the lifetime of the project moved into the newly established Office of Energy R&D Policy, and thus into the very center of the topic, gave the undertaking a special kind of zest that made it fun as well as work.

Hans H. Landsberg
Director, Energy and
Minerals Program
Resources for the Future

September 1974

PART I

ENERGY RESEARCH AND DEVELOPMENT POLICY IN THE UNITED STATES:

AN ECONOMIST'S VIEW

Chapter 1

INTRODUCTION

Signs of trouble began to appear before the Yom Kippur War and
the Arab oil embargo of 1973. The inability of new homeowners to
obtain natural gas connections, the occasional failure of electric
utilities to meet peak loads during the hot summer months, the inter-
mittent threats of a gasoline or home heating oil shortage, the quotas
on domestic production of crude oil equal to 100 percent of capacity,
the closing of aluminum potlines in the Northwest--all pointed to
possible energy shortages.

But it was the war and the embargo, followed by the large price
increases unilaterally imposed by oil exporting countries, that made
most Americans abruptly aware of their energy problems. For the first
time since World War II, the country faced the prospect of gas rationing,
reduced speed limits, and year-round daylight saving time. The price
of gasoline, fuel oil, and other forms of energy rose sharply, and
homeowners were required by government regulations to lower thermostats.
Some industries were badly hurt as well. When the buying habits of
automobile owners changed, seemingly overnight, that industry was
forced to lay off tens of thousands of workers and to retool for the
production of smaller cars. The aluminum industry, heavily dependent
on electric power, is still pondering its future.

In searching for a culprit, one can attribute little of the blame
to the exhaustion of energy resources. Proved reserves throughout the

4

world for all major sources of energy are as large today as ever,[1] and could last for decades if not centuries. Even within the United States, exhaustion is not the problem. Domestic reserves of natural gas and oil would last for over 30 years and domestic reserves of coal for several centuries at current consumption rates. Uranium reserves are also sufficient for at least several decades, and are based on surveys of only about 10 percent of the land known to be favorable for uranium deposits. Foreign oil has penetrated the domestic energy market in recent years because it is cheaper or environmentally cleaner than domestic alternatives, not because the latter are gone.

If exhaustion were the problem, the symptoms of the present energy shortages would be quite different. Exhaustion takes time. It produces slow, relatively steady, increases in real prices, not sudden unexpected shortages requiring either large jumps in energy prices or rationing and other nonprice constraints on demand.

Rather, present problems arise largely from shortages in the plant and equipment, and in some instances manpower, needed to produce and transform energy. The country has not built new oil refining and electric generating capacity fast enough, nor has it maintained sufficient capability to mine and process coal. The adverse effects of these shortages are accentuated by government regulation restraining

---

[1]Reported reserves of coal have fallen, but the reason for this appears to be the use of more conservative estimation procedures, rather than a failure to find new reserves sufficient to offset consumption. In any case, present coal reserves are abundant.

increases in the price of natural gas and more recently other forms of
energy, and by interruptions in established sources of supplies, such
as the Middle East, upon which the country has come to depend.

This diagnosis is in some respects reassuring, for it suggests
the present shortages could be short lived. However, the combined
impact of the many decisions and policies that produced the present
situation was largely unforeseen, or at least greatly underestimated,
leaving the market little time to adjust. Since the supply and demand
of energy are relatively unresponsive to price changes in the short
run,[1] the dislocation and turmoil have been severe and a sense of
emergency or crisis has arisen.

Public officials and others have proposed a number of actions to
help ease the crisis, including proposals to increase substantially
government support for energy research and development (R&D). Probably
the most publicized is the President's proposal to spend ten billion
dollars in public funds over the next five years on energy R&D. Almost
as well-known is Senator Jackson's proposal to spend 20 billion dollars
over ten years, primarily on nonnuclear energy R&D.

These recommendations raise a number of important questions regarding energy R&D policy in the United States: How much energy R&D
should be carried out? What proportion of the total should the government support? How should government funds be allocated among competing
projects? Who should conduct government funded R&D? Who should pay

---

[1]Some conferees thought that demand is appreciably affected by price changes
even in the short run, and in this regard domestic gasoline consumption did
fall significantly during the recent period of price increases. However,
government appeals for conservation, difficulties in obtaining gasoline, and
the fear of being stranded away from home, rather than increases in price,
may have been the principal reasons for this reduction.

for it? And at even a more fundamental level, what are the appropriate
criteria or procedures for trying to answer these questions? Such concerns suggest that research on energy R&D is needed, and that economists
and other social scientists can contribute to the energy R&D effort.

This study proposes to investigate the above questions primarily
from the perspective of economics, the discipline most concerned with
the allocation of scarce resources. It attempts to demonstrate how
economics can contribute to the resolution of these questions, and
thereby help in the formulation of an appropriate energy R&D policy.
It also raises certain questions or reservations about present energy
R&D policy and the way it is changing.

In pursuing these objectives, the study begins in Chapter II with
a description of energy R&D funding in the United States today and its
evolution over time. Chapter III examines the reasons why the private
marketplace by itself will not produce an optimal energy R&D effort,
and so substantiates the need for some form of government intervention,
though not necessarily government funding of energy R&D. Chapter IV
argues that, before the appropriate means of government intervention
can be determined, public goals and priorities must be established
for energy policy as a whole, as well as energy R&D policy. This
chapter also considers the major shortcomings of government R&D funding
and identifies possible alternatives to such funding. Chapter V is
the final chapter. On the basis of the preceding analysis, it assesses
funding policy for energy R&D in the United States.

At the outset several limitations in scope should be noted.
First, no attempt is made to provide a menu of possible energy R&D projects. This would take the study far afield of its primary objective,
and in any case has been done elsewhere.[1] Second, the study does not
assess the technical or economic potential of specific projects, such
as oil shale, coal gasification, or the liquid metal fast breeder
reactor, though references to such technologies are made from time to
time to illustrate various points. Third, the focus is on energy R&D
for civilian applications. Energy research for military, space, or
other noncivilian purposes, even though it may have some spillover
into the civilian sector, is largely ignored.

---

[1]Among other sources, see: Resources for the Future, _Energy and the
Social Sciences—A Compendium of Research Needs_ (Report to the National
Science Foundation, October 1973); and Sam H. Schurr, _Energy Research
Needs_ (Resources for the Future Report to the National Science Foundation,
October 1971).

8

Chapter 2

EVOLUTION OF ENERGY R&D EXPENDITURES

The total amount a country spends on energy R&D, the distribution
of these funds among various fields and projects, and the proportion
of R&D costs borne by the government are all major aspects of a national
energy R&D policy. In the United States, no one governmental agency
or department has had the responsibility for formulating or even
coordinating this policy. As a result, it has been determined largely
by the interplay of independent actions on the part of numerous government agencies, firms, and other organizations.

This means that there is no explicit comprehensive statement of
U. S. energy policy.[1] Nevertheless, an implicit policy exists, aspects
of which this section tries to identify and describe. Funding by the
government and the private sector of energy R&D is examined to determine how major energy R&D policy decisions have been resolved in the
past, are now being resolved, and are likely to be resolved in the
future. Unfortunately, this approach to uncovering energy R&D policy
is not free of difficulties. In particular, much of the desired data,
especially for the private sector, are simply not available. Moreover,
to anticipate future R&D expenditures on the basis of public pronounce-
ments by the President, other government officials, and industry

---

[1]However, the Chairman of the Atomic Energy Commission has at the
President's request prepared a study that recommends an energy R&D
policy for the fiscal years 1975-79. See Dixy Lee Ray, The Nation's
Energy Future (Report to Richard M. Nixon, December 1973).

spokesmen is hazardous given the unpredictability of the American economy and political system. Despite these limitations, this procedure does provide some insights into the nature of energy R&D policy in the United States and its evolution over time.

Private Funding

Individual firms conduct and fund the bulk of private R&D in the energy field. Only a small portion is supported by universities, private research organizations, trade associations, consortia of firms, and joint government-industry ventures, though there are indications that the importance of trade associations and joint government-industry efforts is increasing. The newly established Electric Power Research Institute (EPRI) expects to spend between 50 and 70 million dollars in 1974. The American Gas Association, an early pioneer in cooperative industry-wide R&D, is increasing the research it supports through the Institute of Gas Technology. It is also in the process of developing a comprehensive long-run research program, similar to that undertaken by the electric utility industry several years ago that led to the creation of EPRI. This could further increase the R&D sponsored by the Association.[1]

---

[1] U. S. Congress, Senate Committee on Interior and Insular Affairs, Energy Research and Development--Problems and Prospects, 93rd Cong., 1st Sess., 1973, p. 46. Hereafter this source is cited as The Perry Study, after its author Harry Perry.

One major project now sponsored by the American Gas Association is a four-year coal gasification program. This is a joint undertaking with the government through the Office of Coal Research. Another important joint venture is the agreement concluded in July 1973 among the Atomic Energy Commission, Tennessee Valley Authority, and Commonwealth Edison Company of Chicago to construct a demonstration plant for the liquid metal fast breeder reactor. Despite the growing role of joint government-industry projects and cooperative industry-wide ventures, independent firm efforts still account for most privately funded R&D in the energy field, and are likely to continue to do so in the near future.

Reliable data on private expenditures on energy R&D are difficult to obtain because of their proprietary nature and definitional problems concerning what constitutes energy R&D. Available estimates suggest that the private sector has recently been spending about one billion dollars a year, or perhaps slightly more, on energy R&D.[1] Table 1 shows the distribution of these expenditures for 1973 and indicates that the major portion--roughly 60 percent--have gone into petroleum refining and extraction. Electric power generation, transmission, and related activities have received about 30 percent of the total, most of which General Electric, Westinghouse, and other equipment producers have funded. The contribution of the electric utility

---

[1] The Perry Study, p. 40; U. S. Congress, House Committee on Science and Astronautics, Energy Research and Development, Report of the Task Force on Energy, 92nd Cong., 2nd Sess., Serial EE, December 1972, p. 163, (hereafter this source is cited as Task Force Report on Energy R&D): and J. H. Hollomon, et al., Energy R&D Policy Proposals (Report submitted by the Center for Policy Alternatives to the Energy Policy Project, October 1973), p. IV-3.

Table 1: Estimated Private Expenditures on Energy R&D,

FY 1963 and FY 1973[a]

	FY 1963		FY 1973	
	Millions of Dollars[b]	Percent of Total	Millions of Dollars	Percent of Total
Petroleum and Natural Gas	469	55	600	60
Electricity	371[c]	43[c]	300	30
Other	17[d]	2[d]	100	10
Total	857	100	1000	100

Notes: [a]The sources do not indicate whether the data are for the calendar or fiscal year, but assuming the expenditures are for the fiscal year is not likely to introduce large errors. For other reasons, though, these figures should be treated as rough approximations. The source for the 1963 data warns: "Industry numbers are order-of-magnitude expenditures, and any one may include research on another commodity." And the source of the 1973 estimates cautions: "Because of difficulties in definition, the proprietary nature of many industry R&D projects, and a lack of comprehensive surveys associated with energy R&D industry, a substantial error may be associated with the estimated R&D total of $1 billion. Presently, there exists no mechanism for accurate collection of energy R&D data in the private sector."

[b]The 1963 expenditures are inflated by the implicit price deflator for the gross national product so that all expenditures in this table are expressed in constant 1973 dollars.

[c]R&D expenditures on nuclear fission, electricity generation and transmission, magnetohydrodynamics, fuel cells, thermionics, thermoelectricity, and thermonuclear fusion are included in this figure.

[d]R&D expenditures on coal and solar energy are included in this figure.

Sources: Task Force Report on Energy R&D, p. 163.

U. S. Office of Science and Technology, Energy R&D and National Progress, prepared under the direction of Ali Bulent Cambel for the Interdepartmental Energy Study (1964), Table 1-25. (Hereafter this source is cited as Energy R&D and National Progress.)

12

companies has in the past been small,[1] but should increase as EPRI
develops. The remaining 10 percent has been widely spread over many
areas including coal gasification, solar energy, and energy conservation.

It would be interesting to know how private R&D expenditures are
allocated by type of project; for example, the proportion of the funds
devoted to developing new energy sources, to alleviating environmental
problems, to improving the efficiency of energy conversion, and to
creating new products. Unfortunately, such information is not available.

Another breakdown that would be useful is the distribution of
funds among basic research, applied research, and development. Although
no data exist for all energy R&D, some indication of the distribution
is provided by the data for the petroleum industry. In 1970, firms in
this branch of the energy sector committed 55 percent of their own funds
to development, 40 percent to applied research, and 5 percent to basic
research. Over time, the percentages spent on basic and applied research
have been falling. In 1965, 10 percent of company funds were committed
to basic research and 44 percent to applied research.[2]

An investigation of the historical evolution of private energy
R&D expenditures is limited by the lack of data for earlier years. One

---

[1] R&D expenditures by the privately owned electric utilities, which
account for over 75 percent of the industry's generating capacity,
totaled only 46 million dollars in 1970. Their expenditures increased
to 94 million dollars in 1971. See U. S. Federal Power Commission,
Statistics of Privately Owned Electric Utilities in the United States
1970 (December 1971), p. 763; and U. S. Federal Power Commission,
Statistics of Privately Owned Electric Utilities in the United States
1971 (October 1972), p. 741.

[2] See U. S. National Science Foundation, Research and Development in
Industry 1970 (1972), Table 48; and U. S. National Science Foundation,
Basic Research, Applied Research, and Development in Industry 1965
(1967), Table 69.

year for which some information is available is 1963. A comparison
of 1963 figures, also given in Table 1, with those for 1973 shows
that private expenditures in constant 1973 dollars on energy R&D
have grown by about 150 million dollars or at an average annual rate
of 1.5 percent over the last decade. The comparison also indicates
that the concentration of private funds on petroleum and electricity
was as great ten years ago as today.

Just how private R&D expenditures will change in the future is difficult to predict since this will depend on the decisions of many firms.
However, real expenditures will almost certainly rise given normal growth
plus increasing concern over domestic energy problems. In the electric
utility sector, R&D expenditures could increase by 100 million dollars
or more between 1973 and 1975, as more cooperative R&D under the
auspices of EPRI is undertaken.[1] In other energy industries, the
growth of R&D should be more modest.

Public Funding

Federal expenditures for energy R&D, shown in Table 2, totaled
627 million dollars in 1973. Forty-two percent of these funds were
spent on the liquid metal fast breeder reactor alone, and 67 percent
on the nuclear power field as a whole. Significantly smaller amounts
were allocated to coal, environmental problems, and petroleum R&D.

Comparing these figures with those for 1963, also shown in Table 2,
indicates that federal support for energy R&D in constant 1973 dollars
increased by 167 million dollars during the last ten years, or at an

[1] See *Task Force Report on Energy R&D*, p. 163.

14

Table 2: Public Expenditures on Energy R&D,
FY 1963 and FY 1973

Sector	FY 1963 Millions of Dollars[a]	FY 1963 Percent of Total	FY 1973 Millions of Dollars	FY 1973 Percent of Total
Petroleum and Natural Gas	56	12	26	4
All Electricity	385	84	421	67
Nuclear Fission	293	64	356[b]	57
Nuclear Fusion	36	8	65	10
Other Electric	56[c]	12[c]	d	d
All Other	19	4	180	29
Coal	15	3	94	15
Environment	---	---	55	9
Other	4	1	31	5
Total	460[e]	100	627	100

Notes: [a]The 1963 expenditures are inflated by the implicit price deflator for the gross national product so that all expenditures in this table are expressed in constant 1973 dollars.

[b]Of this amount 262 million dollars, or 42 percent of all public expenditures on energy R&D, was for the liquid metal fast breeder reactor.

[c]This figure includes expenditures on electricity generation and transmission, magnetohydrodynamics, fuel cells, and thermoelectricity.

[d]Expenditures in this category were included under the "All Other" categories.

[e]Apparently about 20 percent of these expenditures were for military and space projects with likely civilian applications. See The Perry Study, p. 39.

(Table 2 continued)

Sources: Energy R&D and National Progress, Table 1-25.

U. S. Office of Science and Technology, "Federal R&D Funding," in U. S. Congress, Senate Committee on Interior and Insular Affairs, Hearings, Energy Research Policy Alternatives, 92nd Cong., 2nd Sess., 1972, pp. 85-86.

U. S. Congress, House Committee on Science and Astronautics, Hearings, Energy Research and Development, 92nd Cong., 2nd Sess., 1972, p. 189.

annual rate of 3.2 percent. While support for projects in the petroleum and nonnuclear electric fields declined over this period, funds
for projects on the environment and in coal research increased. Still,
in 1963 as in 1973, the nuclear field enjoyed by far the largest share
of government support.

Future public funding for energy R&D, like private funding, is
difficult to predict, but there seems little question that it is on
the way up. The growing concern over the nation's energy problems has
even the average citizen interested in finding new sources of energy.
Senators, congressmen, energy experts, and an impressive array of other
individuals have testified to the need for more government funded R&D
in the energy area.[1] Responding to these concerns, the President in
his energy statement of June 29, 1973, proposed spending ten billion
dollars of public funds on energy R&D over a five year period beginning
with FY 1975. In the interim, he has directed an additional 115 million
dollars be added to the federal funds available for FY 1974. Nearly
half of this amount is committed to coal research, suggesting that
the emphasis on nuclear power may now be lessening. In any case,
the decision to expand public support from just over 600 million
dollars in FY 1973 to more than three times that amount within a

---

[1]See U. S. Congress, Senate Committee on Interior and Insular Affairs,
Hearings, Energy Research Policy Alternatives, 92nd Cong., 2nd Sess.,
1972; and U. S. Congress, House Committee on Science and Astronautics,
Hearings, Energy Research and Development, 92nd Cong., 2nd Sess.,
1972.

few years represents an important shift in energy R&D policy.[1]

Other aspects of energy R&D policy may also be changing. The
President has proposed a major reorganization of government agencies
concerned with energy. Of particular relevance for energy R&D is his
proposal that a new Energy Research and Development Administration be
established that "...would have central responsibility for the planning,
management and conduct of the government's energy research and development and for working with industry so that promising new technologies
can be developed and put promptly to work."[2] The new agency would
assume the functions of the Atomic Energy Commission, except those
dealing with licensing and other regulatory matters, and most of the

---

[1]Actually the proposed change is not as large as these figures suggest
because of inflation and the inclusion in later budgets of certain
programs, such as auto-emission research, that were not counted as
energy R&D in the 1973 budget. The relabeling of programs increased
FY 1974 energy R&D expenditures from 772 million dollars to 880 million
dollars. The additional 115 million dollars then brought the final
FY 1974 figure to 995 million dollars. See Claude E. Barfield,
"Energy Report: Nixon asks self-sufficiency as nation's goal, $1 billion
set for fiscal 1974 research," National Journal Reports, October 20,
1973, p. 1574.

While these considerations imply that the increase in real government funding may not triple as suggested, it should be noted that the
Jackson bill, which has passed the Senate and is the principal alternative to the President's program, would allocate 20 billion dollars
over ten years to primarily nonnuclear energy R&D. With anticipated
expenditures for nuclear energy, government funds for energy R&D would
average about three billion dollars a year under the Jackson proposal,
instead of two billion dollars a year as proposed by the President.

[2]This quote is from the President's Energy Message of June 29, 1973,
which is reproduced along with other statements by the President in:
U. S. Senate, Committee on Interior and Insular Affairs, Presidential
Energy Statements, 93rd Cong., 1st Sess., 1973. (Hereafter this source
is cited as Presidential Energy Statements.)

energy R&D programs of the Department of Interior, including the
Office of Coal Research. (The remaining functions of the Department
of Interior are to be transferred to the new Department of Energy
and Natural Resources.) This change would greatly reduce the decen-
tralization of decision making on energy R&D matters that now
characterizes American policy.

Another aspect of energy R&D policy coming under increasing
scrutiny is the question of financing the government's contribution.
In the past, funds have come from general revenues and the general
taxpayer. However, inflationary pressures have in recent years con-
strained increases in the budget, and caused those advocating greater
public support for energy R&D to look elsewhere for possible sources
of funds. One suggestion receiving attention is a special tax on
energy consumption.[1]

Total Funding

Expenditures in constant 1973 dollars on energy R&D funded by
the private sector, the government, and both combined are shown
in Table 3 for 1963, 1973, and 1975. Private expenditures for
1975 were estimated on the assumption that the private sector would
increase its annual R&D expenditures in real terms by 10 percent
between 1973 and 1975 and that the electric utilities would, in addition,

---

[1] See Task Force Report on Energy R&D, p. 195.

Table 3: Private, Public, and Total Expenditure for Energy R&D,
Fiscal 1963, 1973, and 1975

| | Millions of Dollars[a] | | | Average Annual Rate of Growth in Percent Between: | |
	FY 1963	FY 1973	FY 1975	FY 1963-73	FY 1973-75
Private Expenditure	857	1000	1200[b]	1.5	9.5
Public Expenditure	460	627	1389[c]	3.2	48.8
Total Energy R&D	1317	1627	2589	2.1	26.1

Notes: [a]All expenditures are expressed in constant 1973 dollars. The implicit price deflator for the gross national product was used to inflate the 1963 data and deflate the 1975 data. It was assumed that the implicit price deflator would increase at an annual rate of 6 percent over the 1973-75 period.

[b]This figure is an estimate based on the assumption that real expenditures on energy R&D by private firms increase by 10 percent between 1973 and 1975, and that electric utilities, in addition, increase their real expenditures by 100 million dollars.

[c]This figure assumes that the government will spend 1572 million dollars in FY 1975.

increase their annual contributions to EPRI by 100 million dollars.
These assumptions imply that private expenditures will grow at an average
annual rate of 9.5 percent over this two year period, which is slightly
more than six times the rate of growth over the last decade.

Public expenditures for FY 1975 are calculated on the assumption
that the government will spend 1572 million dollars on energy R&D in
that year, as the chairman of the Atomic Energy Commission has recommended to the President,[1] and that over the next several years the
rate of inflation will average six percent a year. If these assumptions are realized, the annual rate of growth in real government
expenditures will increase 49 percent a year between 1973 and 1975.
This is a 15-fold increase over the average annual growth rate of the
past ten years.

Doubling the government contribution between 1973 and 1975 will
increase total expenditures on energy R&D from 1627 to 2589 million
dollars. This means that real energy R&D expenditures will increase

---

[1]After the President announced plans to spend 10 billion dollars on
energy R&D, he asked Dixy Lee Ray, the chairman of the Atomic Energy
Commission, to prepare a report for him recommending how the money
should be spent. In her report, she proposes spending 1572 million
dollars in FY 1975, and 1990, 2034, 2174, and 2230 million dollars
in the four following years. See Ray, p. 29.

In his proposed budget for FY 1975 the President is asking for
1815 million dollars, so the 1572 figures may be an underestimate.
There is also some indication that the Administration is now planning
to spend 11.3 billion dollars on direct energy R&D over the five
year period beginning with FY 1975, rather than 10 billion dollars
as the President has previously proposed. See Claude E. Barfield,
"Science and Technology: Crisis spawns $1.7 billion increase in
research and development budget," National Journal Reports, February 9,
1974, p. 202.

26 percent annually, a spectacular jump over the modest 2 percent growth rate that has characterized total R&D expenditures during the past decade. The jump in government funding will also increase the share of total energy R&D funded by the government from 39 to 54 percent.

Chapter 3

THE NEED FOR GOVERNMENT INTERVENTION

The last chapter established that the government has for some time supported energy R&D in the United States, and is now in the process of increasing its support appreciably. These findings raise two questions: First, why is government intervention needed at all? Or in other words, why will the private sector if left to itself not carry out an optimal R&D program in the energy fields? And second, assuming some government intervention is necessary, how does one assess whether intervention of the magnitude and nature toward which present policy is evolving is desirable? This chapter addresses the first question, Chapter 5 the second.

Most economists, schooled in the marvels of Adam Smith's invisible hand and the efficiencies (primarily static efficiencies) of the neoclassical competitive world, start with the presumption that the government should not as a general rule interfere directly in the marketplace. What products should be made, how they should be produced, and what factors of productions should be employed are decisions best left to businessmen and resource owners.

This is not to say that the government has no role to play in economic activity. To facilitate the efficient functioning of the market, it should provide political stability, money, laws (governing, among other things, contracts, competitive behavior, and the protection of private property), as well as the police and courts needed to enforce the laws. With the advent of Keynesian economics, it was given the responsibility of maintaining full employment, stable prices, and economic growth to the extent possible with monetary and fiscal policy (but

not price controls, at least not on a regular basis). For reasons

of equity, the government may also have to alter the distribution of

income produced by the marketplace.

In addition, economists recognize that individual markets may

suffer imperfections necessitating some government intervention. The

possession of market power by one or more firms and costs of production,

such as pollution, that are not included in product prices are examples.

In such cases, the tendency of economists is to advocate that the

government change the incentives facing private decision makers so that

they behave as if they were in a perfectly functioning market. This

can involve eliminating the market imperfection (or preventing its

development), or alternatively offsetting the distortions that a

market imperfection produces on incentives. In the antitrust field,

merger restrictions are an example of the first approach, price fixing

regulations of the second.

This method of dealing with market failures is reasonable when

market imperfections are few in number and their impact easily under-

stood. But when the imperfections are many and their effects on

behavior complex and interdependent, this approach falters because

the behavior that a perfectly functioning market would produce is

difficult to discern. In such situations comprehensive planning

including the setting of public priorities is often a prerequisite

to determining the appropriate extent and means of government

intervention.[1] This chapter argues that the energy sector conforms
more closely to the latter situation than the former, and considers
the reasons for this within the specific context of energy R&D.

The Optimal Amount and Allocation of Energy R&D Resources

Energy R&D expenditures, like other R&D expenditures, are a type of
investment. Though often more risky and less tangible than other forms
of investment, they essentially are a means of increasing future consumption at the expense of present consumption, just like expenditures on
plant and equipment or expenditures for education or manpower training.

Since energy R&D is an investment, the principles of welfare and
capital theory can be used to identify the necessary conditions for
optimizing energy R&D from the point of view of society or a country as a
whole. Either through private enterprises or government agencies,
each possible energy R&D project (as well as other investment projects)
should be funded up to the point where its expected marginal social
benefit (MSB) equals its expected marginal social cost (MSC). As long as
the extra benefits a country realizes from increasing R&D expenditures on
a particular project exceed the extra costs, the welfare of society can

---

[1]On this point one conference participant suggested the following elaboration:

Past history does not encourage much faith in public planning as
an alternative to the market, imperfect as it is, even in the quasi-
public sector. I think what you are really arguing for is a form
of public planning which sets broad goals but leaves to the private
sector the details and tactics of their implementation. This tends
to be the opposite of what we do in the U.S. We avoid setting any
general goals, but intervene in the economy in great detail on an
uncoordinated and piecemeal basis, reacting sporadically to squeaky
wheels. By contrast the Japanese government is deeply involved in
grand industrial strategy, but intervenes minimally in tactics.

be enhanced by increasing the amount of resources devoted to the project. Conversely, if the extra costs exceed the benefits, a country could improve its welfare by cutting back the project. The sum of the optimal expenditures on each energy project indicates the total amount of energy R&D that a country should undertake.

Although this criterion for allocating resources to energy R&D may seem simple and self-evident, a few clarifications are needed. First, MSC and MSB need to be defined. The former are the opportunities or benefits that society foregoes by committing one more person or one more unit of another resource to a particular project rather than to its next best alternative use. These opportunity costs are equal to the market prices of R&D inputs and are borne fully by the firm or organization conducting the project only under certain, relatively restrictive, conditions, such as perfectly competitive factor and product markets, perfect information, the absence of externalities, and an optimal income distribution. The MSB are equal to the increase in society's welfare effected by adding one more person or one more unit of another resource to the project. Similarly, these benefits are exactly equal to the benefits received by the organization conducting the project only under quite restrictive and generally unfulfilled conditions.

Second, the social costs and benefits associated with a given project are likely to depend on what other investment projects are undertaken. For example, the successful development of crude oil production from shale is likely to contribute substantially greater social benefits if the breeder reactor program fails or is terminated than if it is highly successful. The interdependence of projects requires that a country in allocating resources to energy R&D and other types of investments consider

the MSC and MSB associated with a project given anticipated expenditures

and likely outcomes for other projects.

Third, the MSB derived from an increase in expenditure on an R&D

project are generally realized over a number of years. Similarly, MSC may

not all be incurred immediately. Since most members of society, and thus

society as a whole, have a time preference for money,[1] the stream of

benefits and costs associated with an increase in an investment project

must be appropriately discounted for this preference.

Fourth, the actual benefits and costs associated with an increase in

expenditures on an R&D project are likely to differ from those anticipated

for a host of unforeseen reasons. Given the aversion to risk of most

individuals and thus of society as a whole, the stream of net benefits

associated with a marginal increase in an R&D project should also be

discounted for risk.

Although these complications increase the conceptual complexity of

the criterion for optimizing energy R&D, the major barrier inhibiting

its application is the lack of data on MSB and MSC. Difficulties also

arise because estimates of the risk associated with individual projects

are often not available or are costly to determine, and disagreement exists

---

[1] Nearly everyone would rather receive an additional dollar today than
a year from now or some other time in the future. Among other reasons,
this *time preference for money* arises because a dollar available today
can be invested and used to earn more money.

over the appropriate rate for society to employ in discounting for time
and risk. Because of these problems, the criterion is of little practical
use in determining the amount and allocation of energy R&D funds. Still,
it is of some value, for it provides a useful starting point for investigating
why the marketplace will rarely optimize energy R&D without government
intervention, even though the data to measure the discrepancy are unavailable.

The Private Sector and Energy R&D

Many firms and other private organizations support energy R&D. In
allocating funds to specific projects, these enterprises have an incentive
to increase their expenditures until the expected marginal private benefits
(MPB) are just equal to the expected marginal private costs (MPC) after
both benefits and costs are discounted for time and risk. For the profit
maximizing firm, MPB are equal to the additional net income (excluding
R&D costs) produced by a marginal increase in its R&D effort, and the MPC
are the additional expenditures it incurs in making the increase. So
long as MPB are greater than MPC, the firm can increase expected profits
by expanding its R&D effort.

If all of the benefits of an R&D project are captured by the sponsoring
firm, the only benefits that accrue to society are those that the firm
realizes. This implies that the MSB equal the MPB. Similarly, if all the
costs are borne by the firm, MSC equal MPC. Since private enterprise is
motivated to allocate energy R&D resources in such a manner that the MPB
equal the MPC for each project, the private sector should produce an
optimal R&D effort without government interference so long as all the
costs and benefits are internalized by those conducting the R&D. Or to
turn the proposition around, any valid reason for maintaining that the

government must intervene in the marketplace to assure an optimal R&D

effort in the energy field must identify (a) some discrepancy between

private and social costs, (b) some discrepancy between private and social

benefits, or (c) some obstacle that prevents firms from equating the MPC

with the MPB of energy R&D projects.

Reasons for Government Intervention

In recent years, industry spokesmen, public officials, academicians,

and others have repeatedly urged the government not only to support energy

R&D, but to increase its support substantially. Some of the reasons cited

in behalf of this position are open and honest appeals for assistance from

special interest groups, but most claim greater government support is in

the national interest. Arguments of the latter genre are many and varied.

Some are vacuous or conceptually invalid. Others raise legitimate theoretical

reasons for government intervention, but their significance in practice is

either unknown or small. The possibility that the time rate of discount is

smaller for society than for businessmen and resource owners is an

example. Because of their questionable importance, arguments in these

first two categories are identified and discussed in the Appendix I.

Finally, some arguments are both valid and of known importance. Those

that we believe belong in this latter category are examined next. It

should be noted that some of these arguments, such as those based on

the incomplete appropriability of benefits and imperfect knowledge,

probably apply as much to R&D activity in general as to energy R&D.

Other arguments, such as those associated with public goods and regu-

lation, are particularly relevant for energy R&D, but even these are

not unique to energy R&D.

1. Incomplete appropriability of benefits. The output of R&D is new knowledge and technology. Unlike the output of a steel furnace, an automobile assembly line, or most other production processes, new knowledge and technology possess the unusual quality that they can be sold or given away and still used by the transmitting organization. Indeed, because of imperfections in the market for new knowledge and technology due in large part to their nature, firms can rarely prevent some dissemination of their R&D results, even if they try to do so through secrecy or patents. As a result, the social benefits from R&D often appreciably exceed the private benefits.

This is particularly so early in the technological development cycle at the basic research stage. Here generally there is little pretense of commercial applicability. The objective is understanding, not profits, and results are generally published in technical journals and widely diffused around the world. But even at the development end of the technological development cycle, though the proportion of benefits captured by the firm rises appreciably, substantial benefits often accrue to outsiders.

Some technologies are used across a broad spectrum of industries both within and outside the energy sector. Earth moving, catalysis, combustion, and construction technologies are examples. No single firm or industry can hope to internalize all the benefits arising from new developments in such basic fields.[1] But even the benefits of new technologies specific to a particular industry are rarely captured entirely by the innovating firm. Great Canadian Oil Sands, the Sun Oil Company subsidiary that pioneered the first commercial tar sands plant in Canada

---

[1]For more on this point, see Hollomon, et al., pp. IV-3-7.

30

in 1967, has reportedly lost about 90 million dollars on the project. Now, the company's investment is starting to pay off, and other companies using similar technology are entering the industry.[1] Similarly, the first American atomic power plant, which began operating at Shippingport, Pennsylvania, in 1957, has never been much of a commercial success, but its operating experience has greatly helped improve the design and performance of subsequent plants.

There is another possible reason why the social benefits exceed the private benefits late in the technological development cycle. Firms commit some of their R&D resources to stimulating the reduction in costs and improvement in production techniques that occur as production takes place and experience is acquired. The studies now available on this phenomenon, generally referred to as learning by doing, do not answer a number of important questions. We do not know, for example, to what extent learning by doing depends on cumulative production, time in production, the R&D resources spent to foster learning, and the interactive effects of these variables. Nor is the extent to which learning by doing is transferable known for certain. But the available studies do indicate that learning is important, particularly in industries with rapidly changing technology, but in other industries as well.[2] And presumably some of the benefits are appropriated by other firms through labor mobility and other avenues of interfirm communication.

---

[1]"At Last, Canada's Tar Sands Look Economic," Business Week, January 5, 1974, pp. 42-43.

[2]See Boston Consulting Group, Perspective on Experience (Boston, 1970); Harold Asher, Cost-Quality Relationships in the Airframe Industry (Santa Monica: Rand Corporation, 1956); and William Fellner, "Specific Interpretations of Learning by Doing," Journal of Economic Theory (August 1969), pp. 119-40.

Because the proportion of total R&D benefits captured by the
sponsoring firm tends to increase later in the technological development
cycle, without government support development will more closely approach the
optimal level than applied or basic research. However, it does not follow
that in the absence of government intervention the underallocation of
resources to development in absolute terms would be less than the underallocation to basic and applied research. In fact, because R&D expenditures
on new products and processes tend to be relatively low at the basic and
applied research stages and then increase sharply at the development stage,[1]
just the opposite is probably true. This suggests that the bulk of public
funds used to correct the distortion caused by non-appropriability should
be allocated to development projects, even though the ratio of public to
private funds should presumably be higher in basic and applied research.

2. Public goods. The benefits from public goods, such as a clean
environment and national defense, are enjoyed by nearly everyone. As a
result, producers cannot capture a significant share of their benefits,
and the government usually assumes the responsibility of providing these
goods.

To the extent that energy R&D does promote certain public goods,
government intervention is needed to assure an optimal amount of energy
R&D will be conducted. This argument for intervention is conceptually

[1]For example, a pilot plant for coal liquefaction or gasification is
estimated to cost between 20 and 40 million dollars to construct and
operate. A demonstration plant runs from two to five times this amount,
and a full scale commercial plant, excluding operating costs, from seven
to ten times as much. See Report of the Cornell Workshops on the Major
Issues of a National Energy Research and Development Program (Ithaca:
Cornell University, College of Engineering, December 1973), p. 109; and
The Perry Study, p. 106.

32

the same as that just discussed under non-appropriability: intervention is
justified because the social benefits of energy R&D exceed the private benefits.
However, the source of the external benefits is different. They arise not from
the commercial exploitation of R&D results by others, but rather from improve-
ments in environmental quality, national defense, economic prosperity, and
balance of payments and trade.

Environmental Quality. When particulate matter is discharged into the
air, tailings are left to despoil the countryside, or other violations of the
environment occur for which the user of final products is not charged, the
incentives are reduced for both energy producers and consumers to conduct
R&D designed to ameliorate environmental damage. Those who bear the costs--
for example, residents of a city affected by air pollution--have an incentive
to conduct such R&D, but they are so dispersed and the problems of collective
action so great that rarely do these incentives produce any non-governmental
R&D activity.

The solution most economists advocate for this problem involves government charges or taxes on polluters equivalent to the pollution costs of their
activities. Internalizing pollution costs would correct the distortion in
private incentives against environmental R&D. The U. S. government, however, has not adopted this procedure, but has opted instead for a system of
regulations that allows firms to pollute up to a point without any charge
and then enjoins further pollution at any price. Among other inefficiencies,
this procedure distorts R&D incentives. Firms whose activities are not con-
strained by the regulations will carry out too little environmental R&D, those
seriously affected may carry out too much.[1]

----
[1] One conference participant noted that seriously affected firms may shut down
or move to a new location rather than do more research.

Consequently, under the present environmental program, additional governmental intervention is necessary to assure that energy R&D contains an optimal effort on environmental problems. In addition, the present system requires some government R&D effort to counter the claims that invariably arise that environmental standards simply cannot be met because present technology is inadequate. Failure to refute such claims, under our political system, greatly increases the pressures to relax standards below whatever levels are set down as optimal.[1]

National Defense. In 1972, the United States imported 12 percent of its energy needs. By 1985 this figure, it has been estimated, could reach 38 percent if past trends are not altered by government actions or other factors.[2] Moreover, a growing proportion of the imports is projected to come from Middle East countries. The distant location of these countries plus their demonstrated willingness to cut off oil exports for political purposes makes them a particularly insecure source of supply. Although the United States has alternative sources of energy to Middle East oil, they could take a decade or longer to develop. So in the event of an interruption of Middle East supplies, the economy would for some time be severely disrupted, particularly if the country depended on the Middle East for as much as 20 or 25 percent of its energy needs. Economic disruption would, in turn, undermine the country's defense posture and reduce foreign policy options. Given the public good nature of national defense, the private

---

[1]We beg the question whether levels set down by a political unit are indeed optimal in the economist's sense, apart from the likelihood that we could not marshall the data to make the judgment.

[2]National Petroleum Council, U. S. Energy Outlook (1972), p. 7. Actually, rising energy prices and other factors are already coming into play that should dampen the demand for energy and keep imports below the 38 percent figure.

34

marketplace will not consider the benefits for national defense of decreasing

the vulnerability of energy supplies to interruptions. Some government

intervention is, thus, appropriate to correct this deficiency.

Economic Prosperity. Interruptions in energy supplies, or even large

unexpected increases in prices, can play havoc with the economy. Some may

argue that the private sector can deal adequately with such risks through

stockpiling, long-run contracts, future markets, substitution, and other

mechanisms that mitigate the effects of shortages. Still, there are

reasons for questioning this presumption. A firm that stockpiles oil in

anticipation of war is unlikely to have free reign over the use of that

strategic resource should its dire prediction come to pass. Indeed, it

knows this to begin with, which reduces the incentive to stockpile. More-

over, severe disruptions in the automobile or other industries tend to

percolate throughout the economy. For these and other reasons, the social

benefits of increasing the security of energy supplies associated with

economic stability exceed the private benefits, requiring some government

intervention to assure an optimal energy R&D program.

Balance of Payments and International Trade. The National Petroleum

Council has estimated that the United States could be importing over

30 billion dollars worth of petroleum and natural gas (including liquefied

natural gas) by the mid 1980s if past trends continue.[1] Concern over

where the foreign exchange earnings will come from to pay for these im-

ports has caused many to advocate greater government funding for the

development of the breeder reactor, oil shale, coal gasification, and

other promising potential domestic sources of energy.

---

[1]Ibid., Chap. 14. This estimate was made in 1972 before the recent large
increase in posted prices imposed by the major oil exporting countries.

For good reasons, economists have generally dismissed this argument. First, it is not clear why energy R&D should be subsidized rather than R&D in some other field. Supporting R&D on agricultural commodities or research intensive products such as computers may, dollar for dollar, have a greater beneficial effect on the balance of payments than energy R&D support. Indeed, it may be more efficient to subsidize the production or marketing efforts of the private sector rather than its R&D activity. Moreover, most economists would caution against the use of any subsidies as long as the demand for imports and exports is not so insensitive to changes in the exchange rate that moderate changes in the latter cannot rectify a deficit in the balance of payments. Subsidies tend to distort world trade and reduce the worldwide efficiency of resource allocation.

Even assuming that imports of foreign oil will cost the country over 30 billion dollars a year, the net effect on the U. S. balance of payments should be much less. The oil exporting countries will want to spend at least part of their foreign exchange earnings on American products. And their expenditures for Western European, Japanese, and other foreign goods should indirectly stimulate American exports. Most of the major oil exporting states are developing countries. While historically such countries have not accumulated large balance of payment surpluses, this is changing for those oil exporting states, such as Kuwait and Saudi Arabia, with large export earnings and small populations. But even these countries should want to invest the earnings they do not need for domestic consumption and investment in profitable projects abroad. The United States with the world's largest and best developed capital market should receive a substantial portion of these funds.

Although the naive balance of payments argument has little merit, there are disquieting implications of the heavy dependence of the indus-

trialized world on Middle East oil and rising oil prices for the balance
of payments and international trade. Since the United States is far less
dependent on foreign oil than most other industrialized countries and
since much of the earnings of the oil producing countries that are not
spent on imports may find their way to the American capital market, the
value of the dollar will have to rise relative to the currencies of other
industrial countries. Should the depreciation of other currencies become
substantial, many American industries would find their competitive position
in world markets and even in domestic markets impaired. This would slow
the growth of many industries, and produce stagnation in some. The deficit
in the American balance of trade caused by this realignment of exchange rates
and imports of foreign oil would be covered by the inflow of capital from oil
producing countries. So while domestic production capacity stands underutilized
or grows lethargically, Americans could find that they are consuming more
than they are producing, paying for the difference by selling to foreigners
their investment in American production facilities.

The desirability of this development can be debated. At the same time
it should be recognized that any significant trend along these lines, regardless
of whether it is desirable or not, is very likely to be opposed by restrictions
on imports of both foreign goods and capital, thereby threatening the postwar
trend toward freer trade. Nor is this the only danger to free trade. Other
industrial nations facing serious balance of payments difficulties may resort
to competitive devaluations, import restrictions, and bilateral trade deals.
Some movement in this direction is already apparent. Both Britain and France,
for example, are trying to swap arms and other goods for Middle Eastern oil.

Although free multilateral trade is not usually thought of as a public good,
it is in the sense that its benefits are widely dispersed and largely
unappropriable. Consequently, some government intervention may be needed
to assure that energy R&D adequately emphasizes solutions to the energy
problems threatening trade.

3. <u>Imperfect Knowledge.</u> The private sector may fail to carry out
an optimal energy R&D effort because of imperfect knowledge. For example,
if the typical new home buyer is unaware of the importance of insulation,
or simply unable to judge the benefits it produces in lower fuel costs,
this reduces the incentives for installing the proper amount of insulation
as well as for developing better and cheaper means of insulation.

Since generating and disseminating information has a cost, too much
as well as too little of this activity can be undertaken in relation to
the resulting benefits. Deriving and publicizing the life cycle costs of
the various makes of electric carving knives, for example, may simply not
be worthwhile. Thus, the mere existence of imperfect knowledge does not
by itself justify government intervention. Still there are reasons to
suspect that the social benefits of compiling and distributing information
exceed the private benefits, even allowing for Consumers Union and other
similar private organizations. Also the social costs of collecting
information are probably less if carried out by the government, for it can
require the cooperation of firms. And finally, the government may be able
to duplicate the results that widespread knowledge would produce without
incurring the dissemination costs. It could set insulation standards
that must be met to obtain FHA or VA mortgages, or it could provide
public funds for insulation R&D, in order to reduce or eliminate the
distortions introduced by imperfect knowledge on private R&D incentives.

    4. <u>Regulation.</u> Almost all firms operating in the energy sector are subject to government regulations of one type or another. Natural gas prices, domestic oil production, oil imports, uranium imports, electricity rates, allowed costs of electric utilities, and safety standards for coal mining have all been regulated for some time. More recently, the allowed sulfur content of the coal and crude oil, the prices of coal and petroleum products, and the composition of refinery output have come under government controls.

    Regulation distorts the private incentives for conducting energy R&D. For example, keeping the price of natural gas below the market clearing level has discouraged R&D on new techniques for finding and producing natural gas and on means for conserving this fuel.

    Interest in the impact of regulation on the rate and direction of technological change is growing, but understanding in this area is still far from complete.[1] Since the impact of regulation depends greatly on the nature and degree of regulation, it is extremely difficult to assess the effects of regulation except on an <u>ad hoc</u> basis. Even this approach is plagued by the complex interrelationships among various forms of regulation and between regulation and other market imperfections. The net impact of regulation on the amount and direction of energy R&D, however, is probably substantial.

    5. <u>Market Power.</u> In the energy sector certain firms and governments possess the power to influence prices and in other ways interfere with the free operation of the market. Since these distortions affect the incentives for conducting R&D, some form of intervention by the American government is needed to assure that the country's energy R&D program best serves the interests of its people.

---

[1] One of the few works in this area is William M. Capron, ed., <u>Technological Change in Regulated Industries</u> (Washington, D.C.: Brookings, 1971).

Monopoly Power of Firms. Some industries in the energy sector are natural monopolies, and nearly all are at least moderately concentrated. In addition, many are protected by sizable entry barriers. While economists generally agree that monopoly power reduces production and allocative efficiency, they are far less certain about its impact on the creation of new technology and other aspects of dynamic efficiency.[1] One school, fathered by Joseph Schumpeter, argues that only firms with monopoly power have the funds needed for R&D and the ability to internalize the benefits. Other economists have taken issue with this position. The existing empirical evidence, although inconsistent in some respects, does suggest that atomistic industries seldom support much innovative activity. But at the other extreme, dominant firms, though often fast imitators, also tend to be slow innovators. Thus, some concentration and market power seems desirable, but just how much is uncertain. The problem is complicated by the possibility that certain industry structures may foster too much R&D. This may, for example, occur in oligopolies, such as the pharmaceutical industry, that suppress price competition but not new product competition.[2] So those market structures that foster the largest R&D efforts are not necessarily optimal. This uncertainty regarding the optimal market structure plus the diverse structures found among the energy industries raises doubts that the present organization of the energy sector would without some government intervention produce an optimal R&D program.

---

[1] For a review of the literature in this area, see Frederic M. Scherer, Industrial Market Structure and Economic Performance (Chicago: Rand McNally, 1970), Chap. 15.

[2] See William S. Comanor, "Research and Competitive Product Differentiation in the Pharmaceutical Industry in the United States," Economica (August 1964), pp. 372-84.

Monopoly Power of Government. For the United States the major threat
of monopoly power at the government level comes from the Organization of
Petroleum Exporting Countries (OPEC). This cartel was established in
1960, but only recently has it successfully exercised its monopoly power
to raise world oil prices. Before 1971 the tax imposed by the major oil
exporting countries was under a dollar a barrel. By 1974 it had jumped
to seven dollars, far more than the 1971 landed price of Middle East oil
in the United States.

The exploitation of monopoly power by governments introduces another
imperfection in the energy market. Although its effects on energy R&D are
far from clear, like the monopoly power of firms, it raises doubts that
the private sector if left alone would carry out an optimal R&D effort.
One way the government may try to protect domestic consumers from the
abuses of monopoly power is to stimulate the development of an alternative
domestic source of energy.

The foregoing considerations not only indicate that the private
sector by itself will fail to produce an optimal R&D effort in the energy
field, but also suggest that government intervention on an ad hoc basis
to offset specific shortcomings of the private market is not likely to be
very successful. How would the private sector allocate resources to
energy R&D if the benefits produced by new domestic energy sources for
defense, economic prosperity, and free trade were completely appropriable?
We simply do not know, and have no way to find out. Add in the direct
and interactive effects of government regulations, monopoly power,
imperfect knowledge, and other non-appropriable benefits and the question

becomes hopelessly complex. Consequently, to improve upon the imperfect

energy R&D program that a _laissez-faire_ policy would produce, some govern-

ment planning, including the setting of public goals for the energy

sector, seems necessary.

Chapter 4

MEANS OF GOVERNMENT INTERVENTION

Because the private sector by itself will not conduct an optimal R&D effort in the energy field, some form of government intervention seems justified and desirable. But it does not necessarily follow that the most effective means of intervention is public funding of energy R&D. Before this conclusion can be drawn, the goals of public policy must be clearly established, and the advantages and disadvantages of direct government funding compared with the alternatives available to the government for stimulating private R&D expenditures.

Public Goals and Government Planning

Energy R&D is not an end in itself, but a means of increasing the net benefits society realizes from the energy sector. Thus, the first step in formulating an appropriate energy R&D policy involves identifying societal goals for the energy sector as a whole. In principle, these goals should reflect the performance the energy sector would produce if it were a perfectly functioning market carrying out all activities up to the point where their MSC and MSB are equal. This suggests that the actual energy market can provide some guidance in identifying appropriate social goals, but given the extent and nature of the imperfections described in the last chapter, complete reliance on the market is not justified. Informed judgments, however vague, regarding the costs and benefits can contribute to the debate, but ultimately energy goals must be set through the political process. How much the country is willing to pay for environmentally cleaner or more secure energy must be resolved in the same fashion as expenditures on national defense and public health.

The second step in formulating an energy R&D policy is identifying the available options or instruments the government has at its disposal for realizing energy goals. For our purpose, these can be separated into three classes: government funding of energy R&D, measures that stimulate private expenditures on energy R&D, and all other options. The third and final step involves comparing the advantages and disadvantages of the various options, and selecting the most appropriate alternative or set of alternatives.

Energy R&D Versus Other Measures

Whether the government should rely upon energy R&D, either publicly or privately funded, or other measures, such as gasoline rationing or greater leasing of public lands for exploration, to achieve a particular energy goal depends on which alternative has the lowest expected social cost. This, of course, will vary depending on the nature of the goal. Generally, energy R&D is most useful in achieving long-range goals, such as reducing or reversing the trend toward rising real costs of energy caused by the depletion of conventional energy sources. Similarly, R&D should be helpful in reducing the country's dependence on foreign energy supplies and assisting environmental management in the long run.

Conversely, because of the time required for the development and widespread adoption of most new energy innovations, R&D will rarely be the appropriate policy instrument for achieving short-run objectives. For example, a new, more efficient, automobile engine, even in the latter stages of development, would require several years for retooling and other changes in the production process before it could be introduced commercially. Then, at the rate new cars have replaced old cars in the recent past, it would take about ten years before 90 percent of the automobiles in use would have the new engine.[1] Similarly, if the construction of coal gasification plants were to begin immediately, it would be four years before these plants produced any gas. And, unless this construction had special priority, it is unlikely that more than 12 to 15 plants with a combined output equal to only 4 to 5 percent of the projected demand for natural gas could be in operation by 1985.[2] Moreover, this assumes that the technology to be employed is now ready for commercial use. If instead of the proven Lurgi process a more advanced and unproven technology is desired, four to nine years may be needed to build pilot and demonstration plants before construction on the first commercial facility can even begin.

While not all energy innovations are so heavily embodied in new and expensive capital equipment, there is little that energy R&D can do to change greatly the performance of the energy sector during the coming decade. Measures that reduce the uncertainties surrounding the future of crude oil import policy and the delays associated with environmental regulations may be able to alleviate substantially the bottlenecks in petroleum refining, electric power generation, and coal mining within five years, but more R&D cannot. Similarly, if the country is serious about being independent of foreign energy

---

[1] 1972 Automobile Facts of Figures (Motor Vehicle Manufacturers Association of the U. S., Inc., Detroit, Michigan), pp. 30-31.

[2] The Perry Study, p. 91.

supplies by 1980, high excise taxes on energy consumption and greater
subsidies for the exploration and development of domestic oil and gas may
succeed, but more energy R&D is not likely to realize this goal.

One exception to the above conclusion that R&D can have little effect
in the short run involves social science research.[1] Studies on OPEC and public
policies for dealing with the monopoly power of cartels need not take more
than several years, and their recommendations could conceivably be implemented
within a year. The same is true for research on various aspects of supply and
demand for energy including the impact on supply and demand of different
fiscal policies, environmental regulations, price controls, import restrictions,
and other existing and potential public policies. Outside of social science
research, however, where the focus of R&D is on developing new energy
sources, new methods for exploiting present energy sources, and techniques for
improving energy utilization, the gestation period is generally much longer.

Limitations of Government R&D Funding

For the long-run goals where more energy R&D is appropriate, the
government can intervene by either increasing public R&D funding or
through a variety of measures stimulating private R&D expenditures.
This section, which focuses on the first approach, examines the major
limitations of relying on government R&D funding. These limitations
should be taken into account in formulating energy R&D policy if the
proper mix of public and private funding is to be achieved.

---

[1] This paragraph evoked mixed reactions among the conference participants.
Some argued it deserved much more emphasis, others thought it appeared very
self serving since it was written by a social scientist.

1. Distortions in Motivation. The overriding objective of most privately funded R&D is the development of new products and processes that can be exploited profitably in the marketplace. This objective provides strong incentives to complete projects as quickly and economically as possible. With government funded R&D, the reward structure changes. The ability to get R&D contracts and to please government sponsors becomes important. This tends to shift the emphasis from achieving commercially useful and profitable results to producing difficult and impressive technical advances that may or may not be of great use to society. Even more important, the incentives to produce any results are diminished because a large part of the cost of failure is borne by the government. In addition, a large portion of the benefits of success are inappropriable since the right to patent or withhold information on new developments produced under government contracts is limited.

Even when government funding does produce useful new technology, its commercial utilization may proceed more slowly than in the case of privately funded innovations. This is because the first objective in conducting government funded R&D is fulfilling the requirements of the contract. Demonstrating that the results are commercially useful may even have less priority than identifying further areas of promising research that the government should consider funding.

The problem of getting R&D results out of the laboratory and into use is further complicated if the R&D is carried out in a government laboratory or any facility other than the firm that must in the end

use the new technology. This greatly increases the communication
problems between those who have developed the technology and those
expected to use it. In addition, there may be some tendency for firms
to eschew new products and processes that they did not invent or
develop. This suggests that some of the adverse effects of government R&D funding can be reduced by contracting with private firms
for most of the applied research and development the government wants
to sponsor. At the basic research end of the R&D spectrum where direct
commercial usefulness is not the objective, government laboratories,
private research organizations, and universities should assume a more
important role.

The joint government-industry venture goes one step further in
reducing the distortions in incentives. Here the government shares
the costs and the benefits of an R&D project with private firms. If
the firms involved are those that will eventually use the new technology, this should reduce the communication problems, the "not-
invented-here" bias, and other barriers to the rapid introduction of
new technology. At the same time, the costs of failure and the benefits
of success to the firm are increased. Indeed, if the government participation in the project is small, the incentive structure approximates
that found with private R&D efforts.

Another way to increase the incentives to produce commercially
useful results is to allow firms carrying out government sponsored
projects to appropriate a greater share of the resulting commercial
benefits. This could be done by changing the prevailing policies

governing the ownership of patents arising from government funded
research. An intuitive and common response to the question of patent
rights is that, since the public is funding the work, the benefits
should not be given away to the organization conducting the research
or to any other group. This has been the position of the National
Aeronautics and Space Administration and most other government agencies.
The major exception is the Department of Defense, which has allowed
its contractors to acquire the patents arising from the research it
sponsors, though they are required to license royalty free any firm that
needs the technology covered by the patents for a government funded
project. To the extent that publicly sponsored research has potential
civilian applications, this policy increases the rewards to the firm of
producing commercially useful results. It also increases the incentives of
firms to undertake government sponsored projects, raising the amount that
they are willing to contribute financially to such projects. This
reduces the objections based on equity considerations of allowing firms
to retain patents arising from government R&D contracts.

While the preceding measures can mitigate the distortions in motivation created by government R&D funding they cannot completely eliminate
them. Nor can the shift in emphasis toward satisfying government sponsors
at the expense of potential users in the marketplace be entirely eradicated.

2. Inflexibility. The development of new technologies typically
follows an unpredictable path. Approaches that initially seem most promising
often fail. Others thought less promising or not considered at all at the
outset eventually prove the best alternatives. As a result, R&D programs
must be flexible if they are to be productive and efficient.

For several reasons government funded R&D is appreciably less flexible than private R&D. First, government R&D, aside from that conducted in government laboratories, involves a formal contract between the government and the organization carrying out the research. This contract generally specifies the nature of the work to be done and often is quite specific about the procedures and steps to be followed. While contracts can be modified, the time and effort involved plus the need to obtain the agreement of all participating parties reduces the ease with which projects can be redirected.

Second, with private R&D where the objective is to develop profitable new products and processes, the market punishes those who are slow to abandon unpromising schemes. Good new ideas must be pursued in order to avoid the unpleasant prospect of creating a new technology that is obsolete at its inception. Government funding, by reducing the discipline of the market, dilutes this strong incentive to maintain an open mind in conducting R&D.

Third, government agencies and public officials once they commit themselves to a particular R&D program tend to maintain that commitment in the face of increasing evidence that it needs to be abandoned or modified longer than private firms and businessmen. The emphasis of the Atomic Energy Commission (AEC) on liquid metal fast breeder reactor (LMFBR) is often cited as an illustration of this point,[1]

---

[1] At the conference opinions varied greatly over the desirability of continued government support for the LMFBR.

50

though certainly other examples abound in the defense field. In part
this difference in behavior probably arises because the day of reck-
oning that the marketplace provides for private R&D efforts can more
easily be delayed and even avoided with government R&D. But the
greater publicity focused on government R&D decisions and the need
for public accountability plays an important role as well. For the
AEC to abandon or greatly modify its commitment to the LMFBR at this
point would imply in the eyes of many that billions of taxpayers' dollars
have been wasted. Better to continue support for the program than
subject the agency to that criticism.[1] Moreover, with continued
support the LMFBR may eventually be widely used to generate electric
power, making it more difficult for the critics to demonstrate unequiv-
ocally that the program was a mistake.

    3. <u>Centralization of Decision Making.</u> Government funded R&D,
measures to stimulate private R&D expenditures, and other methods for
achieving the energy goals of society must be compared in order to
determine the best means of government intervention. Similarly,

---

[1]One conference participant suggested that the following considerations
were also important:

    By the time R&D wrong choices come home to roost, a different
set of bureaucrats is in charge. R&D is something which
requires continuity and "organizational memory," probably more
than any other activity. Organizational memory is precisely what
government generally lacks, and what private industry has.
Another important factor is that in contracted R&D the
responsibility is shared between the project officer and the
contractor. The contractor is always in a position to blame
wrong decisions on the contracting officer. This, of course,
interacts with the short memory effect discussed above to
produce maximum dilution of responsibility for outcomes.

within the government funded R&D option, the expected costs and benefits of various energy research projects must be contrasted. Such comparisons require a high degree of concentration of decision making. But this has its dangers, for a promising project that for one reason or another is rejected has no other possible sponsor. Some have argued that the gas cooled fast breeder reactor has suffered this unkind fate at the hands of the AEC.[1] The pluralism and diversity that characterize private R&D activity avoid this problem.[2]

4. <u>Biases in Project Selection.</u> In allocating funds public officials are likely to have preferences that arise from their own self-interest and biases. Big glamorous projects attract attention and focus publicity on their sponsors. A few large projects are easier to administer than many small ones. Individuals and groups with whom the officials have worked in the past may in some cases get special treatment, while in others they are discriminated against to avoid the appearance of impropriety. Projects that depart radically from accepted approaches are more likely to be considered seriously if proposed by individuals with national reputations and affiliated with prestigious institutions.

---

[1]See, for example, Paul W. MacAvoy, <u>Economic Strategy for Developing Nuclear Breeder Reactors</u> (Cambridge: MIT Press, 1969).

[2]For an interesting discussion of how diversity of private R&D helps smooth macroprogress despite the high risk associated with individual projects, see Burton H. Klein, "The Menu of Technology," in Resources for the Future, <u>Energy and the Social Sciences--A Compendium of Research Needs</u> (Report to the National Science Foundation, October 15, 1973), pp. IV-385-412.

Another source of bias arises from the pressures of special
interest groups. Public officials quite naturally try to protect
themselves and their agencies from criticism. Often minimizing
criticism requires that in making decisions the positions of special
interests be taken into account in accordance with the political
pressures they can bring to bear. The emphasis shifts from the interests of society in general to compromising the conflicting objectives
of the more powerful special interests.[1] With energy R&D, this raises
the possibility that too small a portion of public funding will be
spent on energy conservation and in other areas that do not have well
organized groups pushing their development.

5. Instability of Government R&D Funding. Private R&D expenditures expressed in constant dollars grew at an average annual rate
of 7.8 percent between 1953 and 1961, 7.5 percent between 1961 and
1966, and 5.2 percent between 1966 and 1971.[2] The corresponding
figures for publicly funded R&D are 13.9 percent, 6.8 percent, and
-3.0 percent. Public funding by function is even more volatile as
illustrated by the well-known build-ups and cutbacks in defense and
space R&D.[3]

---

[1] A more extensive presentation of this hypothesized behavior of public
officials in the context of regulatory agencies appears in: Roger G.
Noll, Reforming Regulation (Washington, D. C.: Brookings, 1971), pp. 39-46.

[2] These and the following figures for public funding are from U. S.
National Science Foundation, National Patterns of R&D Resources,
1953-71 (December 1970), p. 2.

[3] Although their impact on total public funding is smaller, R&D expenditures on education and manpower, natural resources and environment,
and in other areas display as much or more instability as those for
defense and space. See U. S. National Science Foundation, Fiscal Years
1963-1973: An Analysis of Federal R&D Funding by Function (1972).

The reasons for the greater instability of public R&D funding are
not entirely clear. Part of the explanation lies in the greater centralization of decision making in the allocation of government funds.
But part is probably inherent in the way the American political
system operates. As the R&D efforts associated with defense, space,
environment, and now energy illustrate, new programs are often slow
in getting started due to the inertia in the system, but once the
momentum develops to overcome the inertia the build-up tends to take
place rapidly. More will be said on this characteristic of the American
political system in the next chapter.

Whatever its causes, the instability of government R&D funding
diminishes its efficiency. During major expansions, scientists and
engineers as well as other specialists are in short supply. This
bids up their salaries faster than would otherwise be the case, and
necessitates the use of underqualified people in many positions.
Thus, part of the rise in government funding does not increase the
real R&D effort, but rather is reaped as quasi-rents by those who
just happen to be in the right fields at the right time. This manpower problem is aggravated by shortages in research equipment and
other facilities. Even the qualified may find their facilities
inadequate. When public funds are cut back, these shortages are no
longer a problem. Indeed, waste now occurs because highly trained
people are unemployed, and expensive equipment and facilities underutilized.

6. <u>Reduction of Private R&D.</u> For several reasons government
R&D funding is likely to reduce the R&D expenditures of the private

sector.[1] First, firms may receive government support for some projects

they would otherwise undertake by themselves. Second, the R&D capa-

bility of firms is limited in the short run, so if they accept government

funded projects the R&D they finance may have to be cut back. Trying

to avoid this by relying on underqualified personnel and inadequate

facilities implies a reduction in the real R&D effort they finance,

if not its monetary costs. In the long run firms can increase their

R&D capabilities, but certain inputs are probably subject to increasing

costs. Certainly this seems likely for scientists and engineers given

the uneven distribution of natural aptitudes for these professions.

Thus, greater government funding may drive up the cost of conducting

R&D even in the long run, and make private funding for projects that

would be marginally profitable in the absence of government funding

no longer attractive.

The government might try to prevent its R&D effort from reducing

that of the private sector by making its contribution contingent upon

private participation. Again, the joint venture arises as a possi-

bility. The government agrees to support a project only if private

industry does also. Now projects firms would not have supported may

receive some private R&D funding. But this is no guarantee that the

---

[1]One might question this statement since the average annual rate of
growth in private R&D funding was smaller over the 1966-71 period when
public R&D funding in real terms was declining than during 1953-66
when real government funding rose rapidly (see p. 50). However, given
the many variables that influence the level of private R&D expenditures,
it is inappropriate to conclude that simply because public and private
funding are positively correlated public funding stimulates private
funding, particularly in light of the a priori reasons for suspecting
just the opposite.

net private effort will increase. Joint projects may merely cause
firms to shift resources from projects they consider more promising
to those they consider worthwhile only because the government is
willing to assume a substantial share of the burden. In addition,
joint ventures may sponsor projects that the private sector would carry
out by itself.

Public Policy and Private R&D Funding

The shortcomings of government R&D funding suggest that public
policies stimulating private R&D expenditures deserve serious consideration as possible alternatives for promoting an optimal energy R&D
effort. Since the measures the government could employ to encourage
private R&D are numerous, this section makes no attempt to review them
all. Rather it concentrates on six areas--antitrust, patents, taxes,
public utility regulation, trade, and government procurement--where
changes in public policies are frequently suggested to influence private
R&D expenditures.

1. Antitrust Policy. One reason the private sector fails to
carry out enough energy R&D arises because only a portion of the benefits
from such activity can be captured by the firm conducting the R&D. If
most of the benefits from R&D are specific to an industry but not an
individual firm, one possible solution to the inappropriability problem
is an industry-wide research effort carried out under the auspices of
a trade association or other organization and supported by contributions

from firms in the industry. This reduces the financial burden imposed on each firm, and increases the likelihood that the benefits realized by each will cover its costs.

This potential avenue for increasing private R&D expenditures, it is widely believed, is discouraged by American antitrust policy. Yet the one case often cited to support this position can be interpreted differently. In 1953 the automobile companies set up a joint committee under the Automobile Manufacturers Association to study air pollution problems created by the automobile. Later, they also agreed to cross license patents in the pollution field royalty free and to introduce new pollution control devices simultaneously. The Justice Department sued claiming the companies were restraining competition, and the case was settled out of court in September 1969. Whether the Justice Department would object to an industry-wide research effort in the absence of an agreement not to compete in introducing new technology is unclear. And even if they did, it is not certain the courts would agree.

There is also the concern that getting together with representatives of competing companies, however legitimate the purpose, raises suspicion of illegal collusion. Since this increases the possibility of an antitrust suit, such meetings are, in the opinion of some, best avoided. While the significance of this for industry-wide cooperative research is hard to assess, it could be important.

Even if antitrust policy does inhibit cooperative research efforts, the desirability of relaxing the antitrust laws seems questionable. If done without greatly weakening the competition or rivalry that exists among firms today, not much cooperative R&D would be undertaken, particularly at the development end of the technological development cycle, since new technological developments can vitally affect, favorably or unfavorably, the competitive positions of firms. On the other hand, if changes in antitrust policy greatly reduced competition, the increased production inefficiency and other costs to society could be substantial.[1] This seems particularly likely if government regulation of prices and other aspects of business behavior increases as a countervailing force to the increased market power of firms.

2. <u>Patent Policy.</u> One way to increase the proportion of benefits realized by firms conducting R&D is to change the patent laws. The present laws restrict the potential profits of patent holders in a number of ways. For example, tying clauses that require the purchaser of a patented good to buy other goods or services as well are illegal. So too are patent pools that eliminate competition. And, over time the cost of defending patents has increased along with the probability of their being overturned in litigation.

---

[1]This conclusion was questioned by some participants. In the words of one:

> I am not so certain that the threat to competition if there is cooperative research is too serious so long as there is strong inter-fuel competition. It always seemed to me the reluctance of the coal companies to fund research unless it derived benefits solely for that firm put them at a considerable disadvantage with the industry-wide sponsorship of certain kinds of research by the oil and gas companies.

While changes in the present patent system are unquestionably needed, whether such changes could provide an appropriate means of stimulating energy R&D seems questionable for several reasons. First, to stimulate more R&D the changes would increase the monopoly power of the patent holder. As in the case of antitrust policy, the cost in terms of reduced competition and rivalry may not be worth the benefits. Second, stronger patent rights are likely to restrict the rapid and widespread dissemination of new technology. Third, for many firms patents apparently are not important in determining the level of their investment in R&D,[1] and consequently changes in patent policy would not increase their research effort significantly.

3. <u>Taxation.</u> Changes in tax policy have also been advocated to increase the amount that firms spend on energy R&D. Special deductions for R&D, such as accelerated depreciation of R&D equipment, have been proposed and undoubtedly would encourage private R&D spending. But R&D expenditures already can be completely deducted as operating costs, unlike investments in plant and equipment that must be depreciated over a number of years or much of the expenditure on education which is not tax deductible at all.[2] Greater preferential treatment for R&D would bias the allocation of investment funds away from education and physical facilities in favor of R&D. Moreover, tax concessions may not be an efficient means of stimulating energy R&D, if the private sector would undertake most projects without this incentive. Still, until more is known about the advantages and disadvantages of this possible alternative for stimulating energy R&D, it deserves consideration.

---

[1] Clair Wilcox, <u>Public Policies Toward Business</u> (4th ed., Homewood, Ill.: Irwin, 1971), p. 166. This contention was challenged by some conference participants.

[2] However, training expenses incurred by firms as well as contributions to educational institutions are not taxed.

4. <u>Public Utility Regulation.</u> The amount of R&D that public utilities fund is greatly influenced by regulation. If all the costs can be passed on to the consumer, the incentives to support R&D are greatly enhanced. Moreover, since most regulated firms are not restrained by antitrust policy and the fear of competition from other firms, much of their support is likely to be channeled into industry-wide efforts. The major example of such an effort is the Electric Power Research Institute which plans to spend over a hundred million dollars a year on energy R&D.[1]

Such cooperative endeavors can be considered as an alternative to more direct public intervention where the government collects the tax and allocates the funds. This raises the question of whether the government should abdicate responsibility in this area. An affirmative answer seems reasonable on the grounds that firms are closer to the technologies and the needs of both the industry and its customers, and so are in a better position to allocate R&D funds efficiently. But the question of accountability also needs to be addressed. An unregulated firm will have an incentive to carry out only those R&D projects whose technical and commercial potential is high enough that the firm expects them to increase profits, but a regulated firm that can pass on all R&D costs to the customer is not so disciplined. Moreover, if the interests of the industry and society diverge in the development of new technologies, such as those that conserve energy, and if the government has yielded its authority to intervene in the allocation

---

[1]This projection assumes that public regulation where necessary will be changed to allow electric utilities to pass on R&D costs to consumers. For more information on the plans of the electric utilities industry to increase its R&D effort, see Electric Research Council, <u>Electric Utilities Industry and Development Goals Through the Year 2000</u>, Report of the R&D Goals Task Force (June 1971).

process, how are the interests of society to be served? Regulatory
agencies can review R&D contributions, but neither their past performance
nor their present expertise suggest that they are particularly well suited
to evaluate the effectiveness of R&D activity.

5. <u>Trade Policy.</u> One major impediment to the development of new
domestic energy sources by private interests is the availability of huge
reserves of very low cost crude oil in the Middle East and possibly elsewhere. Estimates of the price at which oil could be extracted profitably
from shale with present technology range from just under four dollars to
twelve dollars a barrel.[1] With Saudi Arabian oil estimated to be costing
between 10 and 20 cents a barrel to bring out of the ground and around one
dollar to ship to the United States, no firm is going to spend much on
developing oil shale unless assured of future protection from such low cost
imports. Nor will the high prices now being charged by oil exporting states
overcome this reluctance. For potential developers of new energy sources
know that once they have a product competitive at today's prices, the low
cost foreign producers will drop prices sufficiently to assure that their
market share is not seriously eroded. This leaves the oil shale producer
with millions of dollars invested in equipment and R&D on which it cannot
recover the principal let alone earn a reasonable rate of return.

The government can protect potential developers of new sources of
energy from low cost foreign oil by tariffs, quotas, or other restrictions on imports.[2] This means of supporting energy R&D has several

---

[1]Most estimates are between 4.50 and 6.00 dollars a barrel in 1972 dollars.
See <u>The Perry Study</u>, p. 92.

[2]The chairman of the Council of Economic Advisors, Herbert Stein, reportedly
favors this policy. See "All Roads Are Steep to Achieve Energy Independence,"
<u>Wall Street Journal</u>, March 7, 1974, p. 1.

advantages. First, compared to changes in patent policy and some of

the other measures discussed, import restrictions can be more dis-

criminating so that energy R&D, even certain types of energy R&D,

can be encouraged without simultaneously stimulating R&D in other fields

that may not need increasing. Second, compared with direct government

funding of R&D, import restrictions leave the decision as to which new

energy sources should be developed to the private sector which should

be more knowledgeable about the technical and commercial potential of

the various possibilities. This increases the likelihood that the

most promising new sources, and only the most promising new sources,

will be developed. Indeed, if conventional domestic sources of energy

can be expanded more cheaply than new sources can be developed, there

is no incentive for private interests to develop any new sources of

energy, and thereby burden the country with unnecessarily high energy

costs.

Tariffs and quotas are among the most widely used import restric-

tions. For some 14 years ending only in 1973, the United States had

quotas on imports of crude oil. Compared with quotas, tariffs have the

advantage that while protecting the domestic market they do not com-

pletely isolate domestic producers from foreign competition. With

quotas producers can raise prices without fear of increasing imports.

Also, the revenue collected from tariffs goes to the state. Presumably

this allows lower taxes or more government services than otherwise,

and so offsets some of the burden in increased energy costs borne by

the public. The same is true for quotas if they are auctioned off

by the state. Some have suggested that this procedure, particularly
if sealed bids are required, would also help undermine the cohesive-
ness of the OPEC cartel. Another suggestion is to allocate quotas to
exporting countries on the basis of the amount of oil exported to the
United States during the previous year. This would allow the exporting
countries to reap all the benefits of the higher domestic prices; however, these extra profits would be lost or diminished for years to come
if the country refused for political or other reasons to fill its quota.
This would provide a strong incentive for oil exporters to maintain
stability in their shipments to the United States.

The protection of the domestic market also has several disadvantages. Probably most important is the possibility that a strongly
protected domestic market could be locked into paying substantially
higher prices for energy, particularly oil, than the rest of the world.
As already pointed out, the cost of Middle Eastern crude even after
adding transportation costs is very low. Should the solidarity of
OPEC collapse, not an inconceivable possibility in the long run, the United
States could be burdened with energy costs substantially above those of its
industrial competitors. Second, the cost of stimulating R&D by restricting
imports is borne by the public in the form of higher consumer prices. As
a result, this cost is not included in the Federal budget, and therefore
not reviewed annually to assure there are no higher priority needs for
the funds. Third, new barriers to trade tend to undermine the movement

toward freer trade and the benefits associated with this development.

Fourth, import restrictions reduce only some of the impediments to

R&D, not all of them. The disincentive created by the inability of

firms to capture all the benefits of an R&D project, such as a demon-

stration coal gasification plant, still remains. Of course, protection

may raise the appropriable benefits from such a plant to the point

where they justify the firm's costs, even though they constitute only part

of the total benefits. But the existence of nonappropriable benefits raises

the amount of protection required, and thus the costs to the public.

Fifth, the firm that undertakes a demonstration plant or other R&D

project because of the protection provided by the government and paid

for by the people is still free to restrict to the extent it can the

use of the new knowledge and know-how arising from the project. Where

the rapid dissemination of R&D results is essential to the realization

of energy goals, other alternatives such as government R&D funding that

force firms to divulge the R&D results may be preferable to protection.

      6. <u>Government Procurement</u>. An alternative means of stimulating

energy R&D by the private sector that has the advantages of protection

without some of its shortcomings is based on government procurement

activity.[1] Through long-term contracts, the government can guarantee

domestic energy producers a market at any price and of any size that

---

[1]The use of government procurement to stimulate the innovative activity
of the private sector has been recommended by a number of studies,
though most presume that procurement will be limited to the government's
needs for goods and services. For example, see: Richard R. Nelson,
Merton J. Peck, and Edward D. Kalacheck, <u>Technology, Economic Growth,
and Public Policy</u> (Washington, D. C.: Brookings, 1967), pp. 198-204;
and J. H. Hollomon, <u>et al</u>., pp. III-21-22.

it wants. If the government's objective is to promote oil shale production,
it can contract with one or more firms for the purchase over time of specified
quantities of oil produced from shale.[1] This approach has been used in the
past to expand the supply of uranium and to stimulate the development of the
transistor and other new technologies. If the government's objective is
broader, such as assuring a certain degree of self-sufficiency in energy
supply, it could simply guarantee domestic producers the price needed to
elicit the desired amount of domestic supply. Under this program the
government could be forced to buy more energy than it needs for its own
operations. Once the desired level of government stocks was satisfied,
the surplus could be sold back to the civilian market. Or if the government
preferred not to serve as a middleman, it could simply pay energy producers
the difference between the guaranteed price and the lower market price. If
imports are allowed to enter the country freely, domestic prices of energy
would closely correspond to world prices. And the major impact of either
cash payments to domestic energy producers or of government sales of energy
back to the civilian market would be a reduction in imports, rather than a
decline in domestic energy prices.[2]

---

[1]Secretary of Commerce, Frederick B. Dent, is reported to have advocated
that the government agree to purchase or guarantee the price of designated
quantities of synethic fuel produced from shale or by coal liquefaction
or gasification. The Dent proposal recommends that the government contract
for 625,000 barrels of synthetic fuel a day in 1978 and then raise that
figure to 4,100,000 barrels a day by 1982. It foresees the development of
68 synthetic fuel plants by 1982 at a cost to the government possibly as high
as 98.1 billion dollars. This figure, which is believed to be an upper
limit, assumes the market price is 5 dollars a barrel below the guaranteed
price. See "All Roads Are Steep in U. S. Drive to Achieve Energy Independence"
Wall Street Journal, March 7, 1974, pp. 1, 24.

[2]This assumes that the supply of imports is highly elastic. As long as
there is substantial excess capacity in the Middle East or elsewhere, this
seems reasonable whether oil is sold under a strong cartel that sets prices
or under competitive conditions.

Although government procurement is probably less effective than quotas in undermining the cohesion of OPEC, it has a number of advantages over protection as a means for stimulating R&D. First, the domestic price of energy would be closer to the international price, reducing the possibility that American producers of energy intensive products, such as aluminum, would be unable to compete with foreign manufacturers because of much higher energy costs. This does not mean that increased reliance on domestic sources would not have a cost. It would and the cost could be high, but it would be borne by the government and the public qua taxpayers rather than energy users.[1] Furthermore, the costs of this program would be included in the government budget, so new commitments would be reviewed annually. And finally, a procurement program would probably have a smaller adverse effect on the trend toward freer trade than protection.

Still, government procurement as a means of stimulating energy R&D does suffer from one drawback compared with government R&D funding. Like protection, it in no way obliges the firm to make public the results of its R&D effort even though that effort is indirectly sponsored by government funds. Indeed, in order to appropriate a large share of the benefits, the firm is motivated to restrict the dissemination through secrecy and patents.

In addition, some have argued, within the context of private R&D in general, that attempts by firms to restrict the dissemination of the R&D results lead to wasteful duplication of effort. This criticism

---

[1]Some conference participants argued that energy users should be forced to pay the full cost of the energy they consume including the environmental costs and the costs incurred to reduce insecurity of supplies. On equity grounds this argument has merit to the extent that the benefits of supply security vary in accordance with the amounts of energy individuals consume.

should be heavily discounted. The only way to avoid some duplication
is through the centralized direction of all R&D, and the problems with
this have already been discussed under the limitations of government
funded R&D. Moreover, some duplication is desirable. No two projects,
however similar their objectives, will be conducted in exactly the same
manner, and where one or even many have failed, another may succeed.
Even after a project has achieved its initial objectives, other efforts
may improve upon the results. So duplication not only increases the
likelihood of success, but accelerates the pace of progress. The static
inefficiency of duplication may be the essence of dynamic efficiency.

The preceding indicates that the government can promote energy
R&D in a number of ways besides directly funding this activity. Some
of the alternatives, such as relaxing the antitrust laws or modifying the
patent system, seem to be plagued with rather serious problems. But others
appear more promising. Regulatory changes that allow public utilities to pass
on R&D costs to their customers, if the problem of accountability can
be resolved, could prove an effective means of encouraging a greater
innovative effort through cooperative programs in industries where firms do
not compete with each other and are subject to direct regulation rather than
antitrust restrictions. Similarly, government procurement may be an
efficient means of increasing energy self-sufficiency or of developing
new domestic sources of energy. The important point, however, is that
alternatives to government R&D funding do exist and that for many objectives
they are likely to be preferable to more government sponsored R&D,
particularly in light of the serious inefficiencies associated with the latter.

Chapter 5

AN EVALUATION OF U. S. FUNDING POLICY FOR ENERGY R&D

Energy R&D policy in the United States is undergoing a number of
important changes. These changes, described in Chapter 2, include a
sizable increase in the total expenditures on energy R&D, a significant jump in the proportion of energy R&D funded by the government, and
a greater centralization of decision making with regard to government
funding of energy R&D. In addition, the distribution of R&D funds may
become less concentrated on a few subsectors of the energy field, and
fiscal policy may be modified to secure more funds for government R&D
support and to enhance private incentives to carry out energy R&D.
This chapter, drawing on the analysis of the preceding chapters, assesses
these changes. It argues that definitive answers regarding their
desirability are much more difficult to give than many have assumed. In
addition, it raises a number of questions and considerations that need
to be taken into account and debated in the public deliberations that
will forge the future course of energy R&D policy.

Adequacy of Total Expenditures on Energy R&D

Chapter 3 provides the theoretical answer to the question of how
much a country should spend on energy R&D: Each possible energy project
should be funded up to the point that expected marginal social
benefits just equal the expected marginal social costs. Summing the
appropriate amount for each project gives the optimal total expenditure.

Unfortunately, this criterion is of no help in determining the actual amount of energy R&D that should be funded because the information needed to apply it is not available. Among other things, one would need to know the stream of benefits associated with marginal increases in R&D at various levels of effort for all possible energy R&D projects, and how these benefit streams vary with changes in the mix of other R&D projects undertaken. Nor can one avoid these problems by assuming that the private sector under the benevolent guidance of an invisible hand will by itself carry out the optimal amount of energy R&D. The pervasiveness of regulation, nonappropriable benefits, and other imperfections completely destroys any justification for assuming that private benefits and costs even roughly approximate social benefits and costs.

Many experts in testifying before Congressional committees over the past several years have urged the United States to spend substantially more on energy R&D. And as described in Chapter 2, the President has proposed doubling public funding of energy R&D over the next several years. This will increase total energy R&D by over 50 percent. The experts and the President may be right. The country may be spending far too little on energy R&D, and even a 50 percent increase may be inadequate. However, given that the information needed to determine the optimal level of energy R&D expenditures is not available, the possibility that the President's proposal calls for too much energy R&D should also be considered.

Confidence in the President's proposal is not strengthened by the procedure the Administration apparently has followed in determining the proposed changes in energy R&D expenditures. Chapter 4 argued that the formulation of a rational energy R&D policy involves three steps: First, societal goals for the energy sector as a whole should be determined. Then, the various options available to the government for realizing these goals—government R&D funding, measures to influence private R&D expenditures, and other alternatives—should be identified. Finally, the options should be compared, and that combination that minimizes the social cost of obtaining the stated objectives implemented.

In contrast with this procedure, the Administration appears to have first decided to spend 10 billion dollars on energy R&D over the next five years. At the time the President made this recommendation in his energy message of June 29, 1973, he also directed the chairman of the Atomic Energy Commission, Dixy Lee Ray, to undertake a study that would recommend an integrated energy R&D program for the country. In a later message, he proposed "Project Independence," which calls for achieving national self-sufficiency in energy supplies by 1980.[1] Goals for energy R&D policy and for the energy sector in general were more fully specified in Dr. Ray's report which appeared at the end of 1973.[2] Here self-sufficiency was also given top priority, though the

[1] See the President's energy message of November 7, 1973, which is reproduced in Presidential Energy Statements, pp. 81-87.

[2] Ray, pp. 53-54 and others.

importance of environmental considerations and energy costs was also
recognized.

But even this study leaves the impression that societal goals for the
energy sector have not received careful consideration. The emphasis on self-
sufficiency, in particular, seems somewhat misplaced for a number of reasons.
First, the ultimate objective presumably is to increase the security of
energy supplies since it is the interruption of supplies that creates hardship and turmoil, not dependence on foreign energy per se. Self-sufficiency
would eliminate some sources of instability, but certainly not all as the
recent coal miners' strike in Britain and independent truckers' stoppage
in the United States clearly illustrate. Moreover, there may be cheaper
ways to increase security, such as diversifying the sources of imports or
stockpiling.[1] And, the amount of security associated with total self-
sufficiency may exceed the optimal, given the likely existence of diminishing
social returns to increasing security of energy supplies and a tradeoff function between security and energy costs (including environmental and other
external costs). Finally, self-sufficiency for the United States without
a sizable reduction in the dependency of Western Europe and Japan on vulner-
able energy sources seems of dubious value, for it accentuates the diversity
of interests and so strains the relations between the United States and its
allies.[2] Early manifestations of this tension, such as Japan's abrupt

------

[1]In a recent study, William D. Nordhaus suggests stockpiling oil instead of
developing domestic self-sufficiency. He estimates that with half of the
increase in costs associated with total self-sufficiency the United States
could over the next 20 years cover the expense of buying and storing a four
year supply of oil at six dollars a barrel. However, his calculations of the
cost of self-sufficiency assume that foreign energy sources could be purchased
at competitive prices. See William D. Nordhaus, "The Allocation of Energy
Resources," Brookings Papers on Economic Activity (3:1973), pp. 564-68.

[2]Some participants noted, however, that Europe and Japan would face less
competition for the available energy supplies if the United States became
self-sufficient.

change in foreign policy in the Middle East, are already apparent, and if
allowed to develop could undermine the country's political options and
defense posture.

But regardless of how carefully public goals for the energy sector have
been set, they were determined after the decision to spend 10 billion dollars in public funds on energy R&D, rather than before as in the recommended
procedure. In addition, there is little indication that the government seriously compared public R&D funding with other possible options for achieving
desired objectives before deciding how much to spend on energy R&D.

These deficiencies in approach raise, for two reasons, the likelihood
that too much government funding has been committed to energy R&D. First,
there are no well-organized interest groups opposed to government funding
of energy R&D, but this is not the case for many of the possible alternative
measures for realizing public goals, such as the deregulation of natural gas
prices or an increase in the number of outer continental shelf leases.
Unless possible options are explicitly identified and compared, political
expediency is likely to dictate that public policy follow the course of
least resistance.

Second, the primary cause of the present energy shortages in the United
States, as pointed out in Chapter 1, is not inadequate reserves of conventional energy sources, but rather bottlenecks in plant, equipment, and trained
manpower.[1] Since Malthus, however, the fear of natural resource exhaustion

---

[1] Whether these bottlenecks have arisen largely because of unusual and unforeseen events, because of inept government policies, or because of efforts by
petroleum firms and other energy producers to restrict output and raise
profits makes no difference to the discussion here.

72

has worried many, even though predictions of calamity have yet to materialize.

In fact, until at least the last twenty years, the real cost of mineral com-

modities has fallen.[1] If the setting of goals is not done carefully and

objectively, this prevalent, though basically unsubstantiated, concern may

unduly influence the results, shifting attention away from relieving the

bottlenecks and toward developing new sources of energy. Since R&D is a more

appropriate policy instrument for realizing new energy sources than for

relieving bottlenecks in plant, equipment, and manpower, this shift in

emphasis tends to promote a higher level of energy R&D funding than is

actually desirable.

The likelihood that the proposed jump in energy R&D spending exceeds

the optimum is further increased by two other biases in the political

decision making process. Because of the checks and balances between branches

of government and the bottlenecks within each branch, such as the Congress-

ional committee system, there is considerable inertia in the American political

system. As a result, when problems arise, such as those associated with the

environment or energy, the tendency is to delay too long in dealing with them.

However, once a critical level of public concern is manifest, the system does

respond. Indeed, it then often becomes politically advantageous, partly

because of the favorable publicity, for public officials to deal boldly with

such problems. This creates a tendency for overreaction.

This tendency is reinforced by the penchant of experts consulted by

public officials to overstate and exaggerate the seriousness of the problems.

---

[1]Harold J. Barnett and Chandler Morse, Scarcity and Growth: The Economics
of Natural Resource Availability (Baltimore: Johns Hopkins for Resources for
the Future, 1963), Chaps. 8-9. For more on various groups concerned about
the exhaustion of resources, see: Thomas M. Humphrey, "The Dismal Science
Revisited," Federal Reserve Bank of Richmond Monthly Review (March 1973),
pp. 2-13.

To some extent, this is a conscious attempt to counter some of the initial

inertia of the political system. One may recommend that the government spend

two billion dollars a year on energy R&D in the hope that this will help

provide the necessary impetus for one billion dollars. Exaggerations are also

possible when they promote government activities that serve the special

interests of the experts. Many of those advocating greater public support for

energy R&D are businessmen, consultants, academicians, administrators, and

others likely to benefit from increased government funding. Finally, over-

statements arise because of the natural tendency to magnify, often uncon-

sciously, the importance of one's field. This occurs not only because an

individual has to rationalize to himself the time and effort he has spent in

a particular field, but also because he is less aware of the potential of

other fields. Energy experts may overstate the desirability of increasing

energy R&D simply because they have little knowledge of the potential

benefits of R&D on desalination, disarmament, geriatrics, and other possible

projects outside the energy field. In short, they tend to underestimate the

opportunity costs associated with increasing energy R&D expenditures.

Even if an increase of over 50 percent in energy R&D is considered

appropriate, the speed with which the President and others propose to

reach that level should be questioned. While greater funding can

accelerate the pace at which new technology is developed, there are

increasing costs associated with such efforts.[1] Even more serious are

---

[1] For more on this phenomenon, referred to as the time-cost tradeoff function,
see: Scherer, pp. 367-76; Mansfield, et al., Research and Innovation in the
Modern Corporation (New York: Norton, 1971), pp. 126-33; and F. M. Scherer,
"Government Research and Development Program," in Robert Dorfman, ed.,
Measuring Benefits of Government Investments (Washington, D. C.: Brookings,
1965), pp. 34-56.

the shortages in trained manpower and facilities that a 50 percent increase within a two year period will create. These factors will appreciably increase the waste and reduce the efficiency of the increased R&D expenditures.

Another potential problem that needs more attention involves the costs and hardships incurred when a major R&D effort is cut back. As the space program has demonstrated, the economic costs to society in terms of unused highly trained personnel and psychological costs to the individuals involved can be substantial. The seriousness of this problem for a large R&D program in energy will depend on several factors. First, any tendency to overshoot the optimal level of R&D effort will aggravate it, for as the excesses of the program become apparent and other problems attract public attention, funds for energy R&D will be cut sooner and by greater amounts than would otherwise be the case. Second, the longevity of public interest in energy will affect the problem. If the bottlenecks in plant, equipment, and trained manpower primarily responsible for the present energy shortages can be largely eliminated within five to ten years, the level of government R&D spending sustainable politically could decline substantially within a decade. A technological breakthrough, such as in situ extraction of shale oil, could have a similar effect.

The consequences of too rapid a buildup of energy R&D and of overshooting the optimal level are serious. Overreaction is in no one's interest. Society as a whole suffers from the waste and misallocation of scarce R&D resources, and the scientific and industrial communities that have the greatest vested interests in more energy R&D will suffer

severely if inappropriate policies attract too many firms and too many
highly trained individuals into the energy R&D business.

Level and Distribution of Government Funding

Under the President's proposal, one may reasonably judge that the
government will fund about 54 percent of all the energy R&D during the
fiscal year 1975,[1] more than double the comparable percentage figure for
all nondefense and nonspace R&D. This raises the question of how much
of the total energy R&D effort the government should support. Using the
procedure recommended in Chapter 4, the first step in answering this
question is to identify the objectives of public policy in the energy
field, and then to compare the various alternatives available to the
government for realizing the specified goals. Situations where R&D proves
to be the most appropriate measure can be divided into two groups: those
where private interests will carry out the desired R&D without government intervention, and those where this is not the case. Government R&D
funding is desirable only for projects in the latter category, and then
only after this form of government intervention has been compared with,
and found superior to, policies that encourage the private sector to
undertake the needed R&D. Under this procedure, the level of government funding and its distribution by areas and projects are determined
simultaneously.

---

[1]This percentage is based on the data given in Table 3.

The government, as we have already pointed out, quite clearly did not follow this procedure. The proposal to spend 10 billion dollars came first, serious consideration of how to allocate the funds second.[1] Nor is there any evidence to suggest that the relative advantages of stimulating private R&D were compared with those of public funding in determining the level of the latter. In light of the numerous and important sources of inefficiency associated with government R&D funding, this approach is likely to produce too much reliance on public funding and too little on measures to stimulate private R&D expenditures. This possibility is further increased by the biases in the political decision making process discussed in the previous section.

Concerning the distribution of government R&D funds, Chapter 4 indicated that energy R&D generally is more useful for realizing long-run rather than short-run goals. This chapter also suggested that direct public funding is likely to be most needed when the rapid and widespread diffusion of R&D results is essential and the rights of firms to restrict dissemination through secrecy and patents have to be curbed. But ultimately the distribution of funds should be based on a comparison of the costs, including all social costs, as well as the technical and commercial potential for achieving the specified objective between each project

---

[1] As noted in the previous section, when the President announced his proposal to spend 10 billion dollars, he directed the chairman of the Atomic Energy Commission to undertake a study that would develop an integrated energy R&D program for the nation. He also asked that the study recommend how the 10 billion dollars should be spent, and a good part of the final report deals with this question. See Ray, Chap. 2 and Appendix A.

considered for funding and the other means for realizing the desired objective.[1] Here the skills and experience of engineers, scientists, and other specialists, particularly those with knowledge of the potential of R&D and its alternatives across the entire energy spectrum, are needed.

Another distribution problem involves the allocation of R&D resources to various possible performing organizations. Public policy need primarily be concerned with how public funds are distributed. In the past, the government has relied heavily on private firms and government laboratories to conduct the applied research and development it sponsored in the energy area. In basic research, universities have received a larger portion of the available public funds.

There is little in the new proposals for energy R&D to suggest that this emphasis will change aside from the fact that the research activities of the Atomic Energy Commission will form the core of the proposed new Energy Research and Development Administration. Since the Atomic Energy Commission has for good reasons in the past channeled a greater portion of its support toward government laboratories than other agencies supporting energy R&D, there may be some tendency to move all energy R&D funded by the government in this direction. Such a trend, if it arises, should be questioned for several reasons. First, it may diminish

---

[1]If an energy R&D project proposed for government funding is found to be less promising than an alternative, this does not necessarily rule out the project. Because of uncertainty, public policy may want to pursue several alternatives simultaneously. For example, early in the development of a new technology when uncertainty is high and costs are relatively low, parallel R&D efforts may reduce both the overall costs and the time required to produce a new innovation.

78

incentives for bringing R&D projects to a quick and commercially
successful conclusion. Second, it may inhibit the rapid transfer
of new technology out of the laboratory and into production facilities.
Third, it reduces the possibilities for getting the private sector to
share the costs of energy R&D.

Indeed, at the development end of the R&D spectrum probably more
use should be made of the joint industry-government venture. Such
efforts mitigate some of the problems associated with government R&D
funding. In particular, they raise the cost of failure and the
benefits of success to the firm carrying out the project, thereby
reducing the distortion in motivation created by government funding.
However, the government should ensure that such cooperative efforts
do not undertake projects that the private sector would otherwise fund
itself.

Financing Public Expenditures on Energy R&D

Although the President has not proposed changing the traditional
method of financing government funding of energy R&D from the general
budget, others have advocated special taxes on energy consumption.
This, they argue, would free public support for energy R&D from the
overall constraint of the budget and would be more equitable since
those who would benefit from the R&D would pay for it.

Both of these arguments seem questionable. Since many of the
benefits from energy R&D will not be realized for ten, twenty, or fifty
years, potential beneficiaries and present energy consumers are far

from identical sets. So taxing the latter is not particularly equitable, and taxing the former is fraught with difficulties. Even if the beneficiaries could be identified, some would be unable to pay the tax and others would now reside outside the jurisdiction of the American government.

Nor does freeing public expenditures for energy R&D from the constraints of the budget make much sense. Tied taxes, as the Highway Trust Fund illustrates, reduce the flexibility of the government in allocating public funds to those areas where they are most needed. They also inhibit a comparison of government R&D funding with other, possibly more efficient, alternatives. Finally, the annual budgetary process enhances the probability that government R&D funding will be reviewed on a periodic basis, and modified as needs and other relevant conditions change.

Government Organization

The reorganization of government agencies concerned with energy, proposed by the President, would consolidate the responsibility for the country's energy R&D policy in the Energy Research and Development Administration. This change would greatly increase the centralization of decision making in allocating government funds for energy R&D. Although this may aggravate the problem of promising projects that once passed over have no alternative sources of funding, it should promote a more comprehensive comparison of potential energy R&D projects and thereby improve the allocation of funds.

In fact, the consolidation of decision making does not appear
to go far enough under the President's proposal. While giving the
Energy Research and Development Administration responsibility for
energy R&D policy, it would establish a separate Department of Energy
and Natural Resources to handle other energy matters. As pointed out
earlier, energy R&D is not an end in itself, but a means to increasing
the benefits that society realizes from the energy sector. Energy R&D
policy should not be formulated in isolation from other energy policies,
any more than other energy policies should be determined independently
of energy R&D policy. The dichotomy in responsibilities created by
the Administration's proposal would discourage comparisons between
R&D funding and other possible public policies for realizing the goals
of society in the energy field. This, in turn, would likely reduce
the effectiveness of the country's energy R&D effort.

From the preceding analysis, one should not draw the conclusion
that the changes proposed by the President and others for energy R&D
policy are necessarily wrong. At most, a much more modest conclusion
seems justified: namely, that it is not as certain as many believe
that these changes are right.

But more importantly, this study has tried to demonstrate the
importance of making energy R&D decisions in conjunction with, indeed
as a part of, energy policy in general. The complicated and interactive
effects of regulation, inappropriable benefits, and other deviations
from the classical competitive market make government planning essential

for the energy sector. Government funding for energy R&D should be

treated as one means or policy instrument available to the government

for realizing its energy goals. Moreover, because of the serious

inefficiencies associated with government R&D funding, for many objec-

tives more effective instruments for public intervention can be found.

But this requires that the alternatives be identified and their advantages

and disadvantages compared to those of public R&D funding before energy

R&D decisions are made.

Finally, the study has tried to caution against an overreaction

of public policy in the energy R&D field. Much of the present public

concern about energy arises from shortages induced by inadequate

petroleum refinery capacity, electric power generating facilities,

coal mining equipment and manpower. These problems have been com-

pounded by the regulation of natural gas prices, price controls for

other energy sources, environmental restrictions, and the Arab oil

embargo. Just how long the shortages will continue to trouble the

American public is far from certain. To a large extent this will

depend on how deft the government is in dealing with the causes.

However, the nature of the causes does not dictate that the shortages

last for decades, as would be the case if the exhaustion of conven-

tional energy resources were the problem.

This possibility coupled with the biases toward too much govern-

ment funding that arise from the process and procedures used in

determining government expenditures on energy R&D raises concern

that the nation is embarking on too grandiose an energy R&D program.

Two billion dollars is more than a third of all government expenditures
in 1973 for nondefense and nonspace R&D. How likely is it that the
American people will continue to support such a heavy emphasis on
energy R&D over an extended period? Moreover, the consequences of
overreaction could be serious. During the build-up, resources are
wasted and diverted from higher priority uses. And after the cutback,
highly trained and experienced manpower and other R&D resources lie
idle, or are shunted off to other uses where their capabilities are
less appropriate. Ironically, many of those now arguing most force-
fully for greater government support are among those ultimately likely
to suffer the most from inappropriate policies that overallocate
resources to energy R&D.

PART II

ENERGY RESEARCH AND DEVELOPMENT POLICY IN THE UNITED STATES:

A CONFERENCE SUMMARY

INTRODUCTION

In April 1974, under the auspices of Resources for the Future, thirty-eight energy specialists from the government, industry, academia, and private research organizations met in Washington, D. C., for a two-day conference on energy R&D policy.[1] The conference had two objectives. The first was to review the study presented in Part I[2] to determine where energy experts disagree with that analysis and what important aspects of energy R&D policy it has ignored or treated inadequately. The second objective was to identify important areas of research, particularly social science research, that could enhance our ability to evaluate and formulate public policies affecting energy R&D.

Part II of this study summarizes the major issues and concerns discussed at the conference, or in some cases expressed through letters and other written comments by the participants. Although the topics are numerous and diverse, they can be grouped into the following six categories—distinctive characteristics of energy R&D, the political process and benefit-cost analysis, reasons for energy R&D, the need for government intervention, government expenditures on energy R&D, and suggestions for further research.

---

[1]For a list of the conference participants and their affiliations, see Appendix II.

[2]Part I has been slightly revised since the conference, but the changes are minor.

Distinctive Characteristics of Energy R&D

Energy R&D policy, as the name suggests, is a component of both R&D policy and energy policy. This raises two questions that the conference spent some time discussing. The first concerns whether energy R&D, apart from the nature of the projects undertaken, is somehow different from other R&D. As one participant put it, if the word textile were substituted for the word energy throughout Part I, would we have a meaningful paper on textile R&D policy? In short, is it possible or useful to distinguish energy R&D policy from R&D policy in general?

The second question involves the relationship between energy R&D and energy policy as a whole. Can the two be separated, and energy R&D considered by itself? Or should energy R&D, as Part I maintains, be considered as one of many tools available to public officials in pursuing general energy policy?

Energy R&D Versus Other R&D

Much of the analysis of Part I, such as the criteria and procedures for government intervention in the R&D process, is general in nature and applies to all R&D and not just energy R&D. Still many conference participants argued that energy R&D is special, largely due to the uniqueness of energy. Energy, they maintained, is for several reasons the resource _sui_ _generis_. It is the engine or force that drives the economy. Once used it is lost forever (or more correctly, it is degraded so that its usefulness is lost forever). In contrast most other resources can be recycled, particularly if low cost energy is available. In addition, energy plays an essential role in human existence because of the biological need of all animals to capture free energy. Finally, political liberty, the emancipation of women, and other cherished features of Western civilization as we know it today simply would not be possible without abundant and low cost energy.

Not everyone agreed with this position. The dissenters noted that political liberty flourished without a slave or servant class in the New England towns of the colonial period despite modest per capita energy consumption. In addition, they pointed out that the amount of energy required for human existence is trivial compared with present energy use. In any case, a number of elements besides energy are vital for human survival, so energy is not unique in this respect. Moreover, energy is in a sense recycled every time aluminum or some other energy intensive material is recycled. And there are renewable sources of energy, such as hydro-electric power or solar energy, which is not the case for most minerals.

Despite this debate, nearly everyone agreed that energy is special for two related reasons. First, a quantitative if not qualitative difference does exist between energy and most other resources simply because of the magnitude and pervasiveness of energy consumption. Few commodities other than water and food are as important for our well being and way of life. As a consequence, any interruption in its supply is likely to be considerably more disruptive and costly than is the case for other resources. Second, like gold, modern governments consider and treat energy as special. By this fact alone, energy assumes a significance and importance that few other resources can rival.

One individual suggested that the analogy with gold was particularly apt because the value of gold is not intrinsic, but largely created by the social and economic institutions that man has established. He felt much the same could be said for energy. Others agreed that the amount of energy we consume as well as our perception of energy is significantly influenced by man-made institutions and could be altered through appropriate public policies. Government programs that increase the availability and attractiveness of public transportation and high-density, inter-city housing were cited as examples.

Many participants maintained that a sensible energy R&D policy has to take account of the specific characteristics and features of the energy sector, regardless of whether or not they are in some sense unique or special. They felt the analysis of Part I is deficient in this respect. While it lays down certain general principles concerning the reasons and procedures for government involvement in the energy R&D process, it does not delve adequately into the industrial structures, institutions, demand characteristics, and other aspects of the energy sector that must shape an effective R&D policy.

Several examples of important institutional considerations for energy R&D policy were pointed out. First, people get very upset if they cannot buy certain commodities, such as gasoline and fuel oil for space heating, which the energy sector happens to produce. Moreover, the price elasticities of supply and demand for these goods are quite low in the short run, and supply depends to some extent on insecure foreign sources. Second, all around the world, governments are heavily involved in one major component--the nuclear component--of the energy supply system.

This has created powerful public agencies and R&D momentum in this part
of the energy sector. People are starting to worry about this. Third,
companies in petroleum, natural gas, electricity, and other energy fields
are regulated in a host of different ways. Fourth, the petroleum industry
has international components that influence its behavior in important,
and in some respects, disturbing ways.

Similarly, the coal industry has its own peculiarities--many small
firms, sluggish growth over most of the recent past, and productivity
increases due to the closing of inefficient mines. If one is concerned
about energy R&D policy as it pertains to coal, it is of little use to
think about what the government should be doing without looking explicitly
at the coal industry. Public programs are likely to affect R&D in the
coal industry quite differently than R&D in the petroleum, electric power,
and atomic energy industries. The differences and the reasons they arise
must be carefully considered in developing R&D policies for coal.

Energy R&D Versus Energy Policy

According to Part I, the decision to spend 10 billion dollars on
energy R&D in the United States was made without adequate consideration
of public goals for the energy sector, of the alternatives available for
realizing these goals, and of the ultimate distribution of these funds
among various R&D projects and technical fields. One of the conferees
who had taken part in the formulation of the 10-billion-dollar program
took issue with this contention. In particular, he felt that considerable
attention had been given to goals and to how the money would be spent,
even though this had not been done in one nice neat package.

However, most participants who spoke on this matter thought that the 10-billion-dollar figure was a political decision influenced among other things by Senator Jackson's proposal, and was not in any sense a rationally arrived at total. In the words of one long-time observer of energy politics:[1]

> In the April 18 (1973) message of the President, he said there is nothing more useful we can do in R&D, and we don't want to spend any more money on R&D. Charles DiBona for a month after that was making speeches that we had already increased the budget to the level where we could manage it. And by June, all that logic had been turned around and a decision made that two billion dollars per year was the right number. There is just no way for this government or any other government to have done the logical planning that some have implied was done. And I don't think that we ought to let the record indicate it was done that way. It couldn't have been.

Although everyone agreed that the Administration when deciding to spend 10 billion dollars had not seriously considered the alternatives to R&D funding, several individuals argued that this in no way foreclosed consideration or use of the alternatives at a later date. Moreover, to suggest that a group of people within the government can sit down and determine with precision the consequences of regulation, leasing, taxation, and other government policies over the next five years and how these policies would interact with various R&D programs, they felt, was simply asking too much.

Most participants, though, were much more concerned about the lack of consideration of alternatives. They agreed with Part I that effective R&D policy cannot be made in isolation of energy policy. This is not only because less expensive and more effective alternatives may be available, but also because the effectiveness on R&D depends greatly

---

[1]Since the conference was off the record, quotes are not attributed to individual participants. Because of errors and omissions in the transcript and for other reasons, minor changes were occasionally made in quoting from the transcript. Every effort, however, was made not to alter the meaning of comments.

on other policies shaping the institutional and economic conditions in

the energy sector. For this reason, many considered the proposed separa-

tion of the Energy Research and Development Administration and the Department

of Energy and Natural Resources to be unfortunate.

One consequence pointed out in Part I of failing to compare explicitly

energy R&D funding with other options is a tendency to rely too heavily on

government funded energy R&D and too little on alternatives. A number of

conferees were concerned that this bias did exist within our political

system as the following two quotes illustrate:

> A crash R&D program is made to order for politicians. It
> gives the illusion of doing something about a problem. It is
> relatively inexpensive compared with other measures. And it is
> minimally redistributive in its effects; it doesn't transfer
> much income or power from one group to another. Furthermore,
> one can always find prestigious experts to testify in favor of
> it.

> My view is it is a tendency of the political system to
> invest money publicly and openly in technology and R&D in
> order to give the impression that the problem is being attacked,
> therefore reducing the political flack . . . .
> As far as I am concerned, that is simply a way of avoiding
> the issue. I can't prove to you that that is the case, but in
> my view if I read Senator Jackson's polemics or the President's
> response, what I get from that is we are going to spend 10
> billion dollars in five years or 20 billion in ten . . . .
> And somehow or another, just keep your hat on, everything will
> be all right.
> Now, I think that is a grave danger of the system. First,
> it misleads people about R&D and what to expect of tech-
> nology. And I think it takes the attention away from what the
> real problem is.

92

The Political Process and Benefit-Cost Analysis

Part I concluded that traditional welfare theory was of no practical
use in determining energy R&D policy because the information needed on
marginal social costs and benefits was not available. In place of this
approach, it recommended a procedure that involves, first, setting societal
goals for the energy sector through the political process, and then, identifying and comparing the alternatives available to the government for
realizing the stipulated goals. During the conference two lines of
questioning arose regarding the desirability of this procedure. The
first concerns the ability of the political process to give clear signals regarding desired societal goals. The second involves the role of
benefit-cost analysis in establishing goals and priorities for energy
policy in general and energy R&D in particular. Related to the latter,
reservations were also voiced about the use of time discounting in appraising
the benefits from certain types of R&D projects.

The Political Process

Many conferees challenged the ability of the political process to
give the decision maker clear public goals in the energy sector or elsewhere. The political process can produce agreement on means but not
ends. Should the system appear to formulate a political goal, one should
not be fooled into believing it is really an agreement on objectives.
It is instead a hammering out of some specific language that one individual favors because it helps his district, another favors because he
likes the prospective contractor, and so on.

A related, though somewhat conflicting, position held by other conferees maintains that the political process produces conflicting goals
and does not resolve the conflicts or tradeoffs. American society wants
cheap, environmentally clean, and secure energy. But how much it is
willing to pay in terms of higher energy prices for cleaner and more
secure energy is not answered in the political arena. Consequently, the
decision maker has to assess somehow the costs and benefits involved,
and the information problems encountered in the traditional economic
welfare approach are back again to plague us.

Despite these reservations, many participants suggested that for some
decisions there simply is no way to avoid the political system, nor would
it be desirable to do so. For example, the importance of environmentally
clean energy involves a value judgment, and must be made collectively.
This does not mean that the decisions or signals produced by the political
system will be perfectly clear, nor that once made they will be embedded
in concrete and completely unchangeable. But, there will be signals.
Right now, the country is clearly worried about dependency on foreign
countries for our energy supplies, and the signals emanating from the
political system reflect this concern. Many of the signals are negative:
The American people do not like to wait in long lines for gasoline; tney
do not like year-round daylight-saving time; they do not like interruptions
in their electricity; and they do not like to see their country black-
mailed over its foreign policy. So, imprecise and vague as it may be,
the political process does provide some guidance.

It was also pointed out that the political process should not be expected to produce the same outcome or the same set of priorities as the traditional welfare approach or benefit-cost analysis. The allocation of resources made by the political process is largely determined by the configuration of political power and the interaction of interested pressure groups including public interest groups. Rationality is more often than not used as post hoc justification for the resulting decisions. This tendency is in part inherent in the nature of the political process, but some felt it also arises because those shaping political decisions often do not have access to carefully prepared benefit-cost analyses. The latter deficiency presumably could be ameliorated.

In the same vein, some conferees noted that decisions made through the political process regarding energy R&D are going to be vitally influenced by how the general public defines the issues and even what they determine are the issues. The R&D community can influence the outcome, but it cannot control it. Consequently, if sound energy R&D policies are to develop, the public must be adequately informed by government officials, the R&D community, educational institutions, and other sources about energy problems and the role of energy R&D in alleviating these problems.

Benefit-Cost Analysis

The political process should not be considered as a substitute for benefit-cost analysis. Presumably, each actor in the political process makes an informal benefit-cost analysis based on the information he has available and the issues as he sees them in deciding how to vote and otherwise act on various issues.[1] Moreover, formal benefit-

---

[1] Some might argue that the benefits and costs he considers are those that directly affect him rather than society as a whole. Even if this is the case, he would still be using benefit-cost techniques.

cost studies can complement and interact with the political process. For example, because the country is clearly worried about dependence on foreign energy supplies, the Administration has proposed Project Independence. The purpose of this program is to communicate a sense of urgency, but the specific goals of the program, such as complete independence of foreign energy supplies by 1980 can and probably will be modified over time. Here benefit-cost analyses should play a role. In addition, benefit-cost analyses should provide guidance on what specific projects make sense in reducing domestic dependence on foreign energy, and which projects are totally nonsensical. Thus, an interchange between the political process and benefit-cost analysis is needed. Signals and programs generated by the former should be modified as new information and assessments become available from the latter, but the latter alone cannot be expected to resolve issues that involve value judgments. Here guidance from the political system is essential.

One participant suggested that benefit-cost analysis is more useful in comparing specific alternatives as opposed to determining the menu of alternatives. Others thought that benefit-cost analysis became less and less useful as the issues considered became bigger and their impact on society greater. For example, benefit-cost analysis is probably a more useful tool in assessing different routes for a pipeline from the North Slope of Alaska, than in assessing the desirability of a plutonium economy based on the breeder reactor with all of the long-range safety problems the latter entails. When decisions become extremely large and alter the entire social system, as in the latter case, benefit-cost analysis falters because many important considerations are unquantifiable and involve value judgments.

Time Discounting

A number of participants expressed concern that discounting the future stream of benefits by any reasonable discount rate causes benefit-cost analysis to reject R&D projects with very long gestation periods, even though some of these projects could be very important, even critical, to the welfare of future generations. The following quote from a letter received after the conference illustrates this concern:

> There are some kinds of R&D that are serially correlated
> in such a way that discounted cash flow arguments may be mis-
> leading. It may take so long for some concepts and ideas to
> gestate that one would never start them because their "pay-off"
> is so distant in the future that it has negligible discounted
> present value. Yet if the research is not started now, the
> pay-off will never be achieved because it depends on an extended
> series of events which have to take place in a certain or-
> dered sequence, determined by the logic of science itself,
> which just cannot be hurried up very much by the expenditure
> of resources. Admittedly this argument applies mostly to
> basic research, which I define as research whose strategy
> is governed by the logic of science rather than potential
> applicability, and is thus of such a nature that the area of
> ultimate pay-off cannot be more than vaguely foreseen. How-
> ever, I believe the same considerations apply to certain kinds
> of long range applied research, i.e., research whose social
> objectives can be identified fairly clearly, but which will
> take a long time to come to fruition. An example of this
> kind of research may be environmental studies aimed at under-
> standing the effect of fossil fuel combustion on world climate.
> It may be thirty years before we can say with certainty whether
> present and foreseeable rates of combustion of fossil fuels
> will or will not have global climatic effects, what they may
> be, or how they might be counteracted. Yet we had better
> start as soon as possible because we may have to convert to
> some other source of energy to avoid these effects, and we
> cannot afford to wait until the problem is actually upon us.
> It is the inability to telescope progress in certain areas
> which renders the discounted cash flow approach by itself an
> insufficient criterion. You could say, of course, that it is
> the risk of a certain sort of answer which gives extra impor-
> tance to the research, a kind of downside risk to our whole
> civilization.

This raises the question of whether in certain instances some-thing is wrong in principle with the use of benefit-cost techniques or whether for certain types of research their application is simply difficult and hazardous because of problems in measuring benefits. With basic research projects it is not certain any benefits will be forthcoming, and if there are, their nature and value are highly unpredictable. Consequently, no way exists to even roughly estimate benefits, and funds generally are committed on the basis of the historical record of benefits from such research. This, however, suggests that little attempt should be made in allocating basic research funds to redirect the researcher's efforts away from what he believes is the most promising avenue of research toward some specific commercial or societal objective on the basis of benefit-cost analysis.

The sequential nature of certain types of applied research in generating new technology may also create problems in estimating benefits. Rarely is the necessary sequencing of research known ex ante, and consequently, it is difficult to judge which projects must be undertaken now to obtain the desired technology by a given date. Yet the value of carrying out a particular research project now may depend greatly on whether or not its postponement would delay the introduction of the new technology. In addition, where a research project is just one of many research efforts that ultimately produces a useful technology, a variation of the joint cost problem arises in deciding how to divide the benefits among the various research efforts.

Finally, problems arise in measuring the benefits of research projects that are in essence insurance policies protecting society from some catastrophe whose probability of occurrence is very low. If the cost of the catastrophe is not known precisely but is very, very high, and the probability of the catastrophe occurring is not known precisely but is very, very low, what is the appropriate value to assign to such insurance? There simply is

no way to calculate a specific number. The essence of the problem, however, lies in our inability to quantify the benefits, and not in discounting.
If the cost to society of the catastrophe is infinitely large and the probability of its occurrence is not infinitely small, the insurance that research
can provide will be justified by benefit-cost analysis regardless of the
discount rate or the long-run nature of the problem.

The preceding suggests that benefit-cost analysis is not for conceptual reasons inapplicable in certain situations, but rather that reliable information on the benefits (and possibly costs and discount rate)
needed to use this analytical tool may not always exist. Here, as in the
case of value judgments discussed above, the political process must provide
guidance as to how to assess the benefits and costs.

Reasons for Energy R&D

In producing and using energy, tradeoffs can be made between the
monetary (internalized) costs, the environmental and other external costs,
and the security of supplies from unanticipated interruption. For example,
the security of American energy supplies can be increased by relying more
heavily on higher cost domestic sources. Similarly, environmentally
cleaner energy is possible, if the United States is willing to pay more
for its energy or to rely more extensively on less secure foreign supplies.
At any particular time this tradeoff relationship (which can be conceived
of as a surface in a three dimension diagram with monetary costs, environmental costs and other externalities, and security measured on the
three axes) is fixed largely by state of technology, the quantity and
quality of energy reserves available in the United States and abroad,
and the prevailing political and economic institutions.

Over time, the tradeoff surface can shift. The depletion of high
grade or easy to find energy resources tends to shift the surface outward
causing monetary costs to increase for any given level of environmental
costs and security. Institutional changes, such as the formation of OPEC,
can also increase monetary costs and reduce security. Conversely, the
development and introduction of cost reducing technology pushes the tradeoff surface in the opposite direction.

Part I contends that energy R&D is an effective means of countering
those forces, such as the depletion of energy resources, that tend to shift
the tradeoff surface outward and to increase the cost or insecurity of
energy over the long run. Due to the time required for energy R&D to generate useful technology and for the latter to be widely adopted, Part I

maintains that energy R&D is of little use in dealing with short-run problems that are likely to be resolved in five or ten years. In addition,
it argues that the depletion or exhaustion of energy resources, if a
problem at all, is a long-run problem—not an immediate problem—and has
nothing to do with our current energy difficulties. The latter instead
arise primarily from shortages in plant, equipment, and trained manpower
that quite conceivably could be eliminated within a decade.

During the conference, this analysis was challenged for three reasons—
inadequate concern for the problems created by exhaustion, apparent neglect
of other potential long-run problems besides exhaustion, and failure to
recognize that certain kinds of energy R&D can produce significant short-
run benefits.

Exhaustion

Criticism over the role ascribed to exhaustion in Part I was of three
types. First, a few conferees maintained that exhaustion is a problem
today and is, Part I notwithstanding, a significant cause of our present
energy difficulties. This line of argument, which was not widely supported,
rests primarily on the present reserve situation in the domestic natural
gas industry.

Second, a number of participants felt that Part I overemphasizes the
importance of plant, equipment, and personnel bottlenecks, particularly
with respect to petroleum refinery capacity. They noted that refinery
capacity has been increasing rapidly over the last several years particularly if the capacity built in the Caribbean specifically for the
American market is considered. Moreover, during the latter part of 1973
and the early months of 1974, refineries ran at less than full capacity.

According to one individual, the jump in refinery capacity during 1973
was largely due to government regulations that allocated the available
crude among companies on the basis of their refinery capacities. As a
result, a firm could increase its share by postponing planned refinery
retirements and by accelerating the construction of new facilities.
Another participant with first-hand experience in the refinery business,
however, contended that the most additions to refinery capacity had come
earlier in 1973 before the government allocation program when a genuine
shortage of capacity existed. In his words,

> . . . the people I knew were working like dogs to get
> what they could out of existing equipment. And they found
> ways that they simply had not recognized before. And there
> was much increase that just came about from what we call
> bottleneck removal and stretching.

The latter suggests that, although refinery capacity may be more elastic
in the short run than many suppose, it nevertheless has been a bottleneck.

Third, although most participants did not attribute current energy
problems to exhaustion, many considered it a serious long-run problem.
One even suggested the United States and other industrial countries
were in danger of suffering the same kind of stagnation that befell the
Mediterranean cultures when they ran out of fuel wood during the Roman
period.

In this respect, many thought that Part I was misleading. They
noted that comparing current consumption with present reserves gives an
overly optimistic picture of the adequacy of reserves since consumption
has, at least until recently, been growing rapidly. Moreover, in some
respects it is more meaningful to compare present consumption with
reserve additions rather than reserves. And the rate of finding new
oil and gas reserves in the United States, until recently, has not kept
pace with consumption.

Nor were all conferees comforted by our ability in the past to cope with the exhaustion problem despite recurring alarm over this problem. As the following comments written by two participants after the conference illustrate:

> I am not impressed by the many citations of the crying of "Wolf," in years past. I am well aware from reading internal private company reports that in the mid-twenties it was expected that petroleum would run out in ten years. However, much has changed in the years since then, including improvements in geology and the fact that the exponential rise in energy use has led to a situation where the incremental amounts of energy used each year have become stupendous. Thus to me the important question is not what happened in 1973, but what will happen in the period ten to twenty years from now.

> I suspect that most technologists such as myself look on the fuel supply situation in 1973 as merely a triggering event to mobilize manpower and resources in an attempt to avoid the real energy crunch which we expect to come as much as ten years later. Thus it gets us started doing things that we believed we would have to do anyway but were afraid could not be done fast enough if we waited until the real crisis hit us.

Not all conferees, however, were so concerned about the exhaustion problem. Some thought it likely that substantial new reserves would be found in the United States and abroad as a result of the recent jumps in energy prices. In support of this possibility, they pointed to the recent surge in exploration activity. Moreover, in the long run they saw no reason for assuming that technology would not find new energy sources to replace those we are now depleting. And some possible new sources, such as solar power or fusion, are for all practical purposes inexhaustible. While few holding this position were prepared to argue that the real cost of energy would not in the long run rise above the levels prevailing in the early seventies, they did not feel increases would be large enough to cause economic stagnation or a painful readjustment towards a much less energy intensive standard of living.

In general, the economists were less concerned about the consequences

of exhaustion than the scientists and technologists, but the lines were

not drawn entirely along disciplines. Apparently, exhaustion is an im-

portant issue over which energy specialists sharply disagree.

Other Long-run Problems

Part I appears to emphasize the tendency of energy costs to rise

due to the depletion of high grade energy resources as the long-run prob-

lem par excellence, and thus the principal problem on which R&D should

focus. At the conference several individuals pointed out that other

long-run problems also existed and deserved R&D attention. Among the

examples cited were reconciling energy use with environmental objectives

and dealing with supply interruptions. On this point there was no

opposition.

Short-term Benefits

But considerable disagreement did arise over whether R&D, aside from

social science research, could produce sizable benefits in the energy

sector in the short run, contrary to the contention of Part I. Ambiguity

over what R&D encompassed was in part responsible for this debate. R&D

defined to include all technical activity to improve technology--including

activities such as troubleshooting and changes on the work floor involving

modifications of machinery, processes, and material flows--can obviously

have important short-run benefits. However, for purposes of data collection

and policy formulation R&D generally is not so broadly defined. Moreover,

as some participants noted, troubleshooting and other technical activities with quick payoffs are probably best left to firms, in part because firms are much closer to the problems needing attention and in part because almost all of the benefits from this type of activity can be captured by the sponsoring firm.

Even when R&D was defined narrowly, some conferees felt that Part I was too pessimistic about the potential short-run benefits, particularly in conservation and on the demand side of energy in general. They noted that at any particular time R&D projects are in various stages of development, and some of the more advanced projects presumably can be brought to fruition relatively quickly. Other participants, however, took issue with this position citing the time it takes to get most significant new energy innovations into widespread use. This, they argued, is true for innovations affecting the demand as well as the supply of energy. For example, if an improved automobile engine consuming considerably less gasoline were developed, on the basis of past experience it would take ten years or longer to replace the present stock of American automobiles possessing older, less efficient, engines.

The Need for Government Intervention

On a number of occasions the conference turned its attention to the reasons for government intervention in energy R&D activity. In addition to externalities and the considerations of traditional welfare economics discussed in Part I and Appendix I, a number of participants argued that the government had an obligation to mitigate the adverse effects of major changes in public policy, such as the rising monetary and environmental costs associated with Project Independence. Others felt that public support for energy R&D should be used as a strategic tool in bargaining with the Arabs and others threatening to cut off our energy supplies or to increase prices appreciably through cartel activity. Finally, several participants expressed the opinion that the government should not support energy R&D at the advanced stages of development. One or two even questioned whether government intervention in early stages of the R&D process was desirable.

Externalities and Other Traditional Welfare Considerations

There was general agreement among the conferees that the inappropriability of many benefits flowing from R&D activity--energy R&D as well as other R&D--would in the absence of government support keep the level of such activity below the optimum. Nor did anyone object to the contention of Part I that government regulation, market power, and imperfect knowledge are ubiquitous in the energy sector and significantly distort R&D incentives.

When opposition to Part I arose, it centered on the reasons for government intervention that Part I considers of unknown or dubious importance. In the opinion of many participants, the availability of funds is a serious problem inhibiting private support for a number of expensive but important projects. Considering IBM unique among firms in its ability to raise funds, they were not convinced by the reference to this firm's expenditure on its 360 series of computers. Others argued that the atomistic market structure in coal and electric power, by inhibiting access to sufficient funding, has retarded an adequate R&D effort in these industries.

Still others pointed out that the private sector could not be expected to support fusion research and other projects involving a very high risk. The reasons why the government should fund such projects were not completely spelled out, but, in addition to the inappropriability of benefits, the greater ability of the government to pool risks was considered important. Some supporters of this position also believe that the rate of risk discount is greater for firms than for society in general. In this and other contexts, one person suggested that individuals may perceive the probability distributions of success differently. If society in general is more optimistic about the prospects for a project than the firms capable of carrying out the project and if this optimism is not based on ignorance, this provides an additional justification for public support for certain high risk projects.

As already noted, many people had reservations about time discounting for potentially vital R&D projects with long gestation periods. In addition, some expressed the belief that the rate of time discount for society is and should be lower than that of private firms. They found the a priori arguments in Appendix I suggesting that the discount rate for firms could be either less than or greater than the rate for society superficial.

After the conference, one participant raised the question of whether differences in discount rates matter.

> The pay-out of the investment in R&D is not in the same time-frame as the evaluation of the decisionmakers' own performance. If as a corporate executive I have to show some "results" by next year's board meeting, the nature of the R&D project I choose cannot be adequately evaluated by a discount rate. I might choose a ten year project that will have detectable results in the first year of effort over a five year project that cannot be evaluated at all until it is completed. The same would be true of the government politician or administrator.

This comment suggests we still have much to learn regarding how time influences R&D decisions and the need for government intervention as a result of the possible distortions this produces.

Major Changes in Government Policies

When the government makes a major change in policy, such as the recent commitment reflected in Project Independence to increase self-sufficiency in energy supplies, there are likely to be political, social, and economic costs associated with such decisions. In the case of Project Independence, the environmental and monetary costs of energy are likely to rise. Many conferees felt that the government has a responsibility to alleviate such adverse effects through R&D support as well as other means.

This justification for government support for energy R&D was vigorously contested however.

> The question you have to ask relative to anything like Project Independence is how much are you willing to pay to do something in order to reduce the consequences of a sudden disruption or reduction in supply? Now, obviously, that is a social, political, economic decision that has to be made essentially on a national political basis.

Having decided that question, you then have to limit imports in some way—by setting rules, putting up fences, providing variable tariffs, or whatever means you wish. If you then do not control prices in the economy, the problem reduces to what do you do about increased supply costs in the short and long run.

In the short run, that is within ten to fifteen years, R&D is not going to have much impact on supply. Nor will it greatly affect demand. Prices, rationing, or some other vehicle will be necessary to equilibrate supply and demand and reduce queues if you put a barrier around the country.

In the long run, the question is, will the private sector provide the desired amount of technological effort, economic development, or whatever is required to increase supply or reduce demand? The reasons why it may not we have already discussed and do not depend on the level of imports. I see no difference, therefore, in the question of what R&D should be done, and whether industry should do it, in the long term between the case where you open the gates to imports or where you close the gates to imports. I do not see any logical difference between these two problems.

While agreeing in principle with the above remarks, another participant questioned their usefulness. He pointed out that conditions in the domestic energy markets would be enormously different under Project Independence compared with a relatively free import policy, and that these differences have major implications, first, for the role of R&D and, second, for the role of the government in the organization and financing of that R&D.

Although the conference returned to this question on a number of occasions, a consensus was never reached as to whether changes in government goals and policy by themselves justify government support for R&D. There was, however, no disagreement over the fact that Project Independence and other changes in public policy could greatly affect economic conditions in the energy sector and thereby alter the incentives for private R&D and the need for government R&D support.

Bargaining Power

The OPEC countries by joining together and forming a cartel have greatly increased the amount of economic rents they realize on their petroleum production. Moreover, they have at times threatened to cut off the supply of oil to the United States and other importing countries in order to extract political concessions. To counteract this type of behavior, the United States and other petroleum importing countries need to increase their countervailing bargaining power. This might be done by forming an Organization of Petroleum Importing Countries or in any number of other ways.

In this regard, a number of conferees thought that energy R&D policy could be used for bargaining or strategic purposes. Specifically, the United States could develop, or threaten to develop, new domestic sources of energy. Since the American market imports substantial amounts of petroleum, exporting countries presumably do not want to lose this market and will make concessions to avoid this possibility. This strategy would require government R&D funding since the new technologies and new sources of energy are unlikely to be competitive with low-cost foreign oil, and may never be used.

Others questioned this line of reasoning. First, they pointed out, given the time required for R&D to produce major new sources of energy, it is unlikely that this ploy would appreciably alter OPEC's behavior. For this reason, the expansion of domestic energy production using existing technology would seem to make more sense. Moreover, for the threat to be credible, it would not only be necessary to have the technology but also the required plant and equipment ready for use. This, in addition to aggravating the time problem, would be expensive. And, to the extent that the cost of energy from the new sources exceeded the cost of producing crude oil abroad, foreign producers could still collect economic rents unless Americans were also prepared to underwrite more costly domestic sources. Finally, several individuals questioned the value of self-sufficiency for the United States as long as Western Europe and Japan were heavily dependent on imported oil.

Problems with Government Intervention

Although no one argued that the private sector by itself would carry out an adequate energy R&D effort, several individuals expressed concern about the desirability of government intervention at certain stages of the R&D cycle. Indeed, one person even questioned whether the government should intervene at all. He felt that a thorough study of past government support for R&D just might find that on balance the costs of such efforts exceeded the benefits due to the waste and mismanagement associated with public R&D efforts.

While no one else espoused this position, several participants did feel that the government should not support, either by R&D subsidies or by guaranteed prices, pilot or demonstration plants. Once this commitment is made, if the private sector fails to pick up the government's initiative, strong pressure arises for the government to continue-- building the first commercial facility and even engaging in commercial operation. If the government were more adept than the private sector at identifying good technology--good in terms of its technical and commercial potential--this might not be a problem. But most of those who discussed this issue felt strongly that just the opposite was the case.

A related problem bothering a number of participants was the relative
inflexibility of government R&D support.

> Once the government takes on a major responsibility for
> funding an R&D program, and once it gets a strong advocate
> agency to stand behind that program (and that agency builds
> up a constituency of its own), then certain things which
> you may have thought of in the early stages of the game as
> options, no longer are options. You get locked in.

Another individual supporting the same point noted that whenever the
government runs a funding program there are certain pressures, particularly
in the congressional appropriations process, to regularize the distribution of funds. This has the benefit of stabilizing government funding,
identified as a problem with government R&D support in Part I, but it
also means that the distribution of funds among projects may bear only
the slightest relationship to what a benefit-cost analysis would recommend.

The flexibility problem may be most severe when the government not
only funds the R&D effort but also conducts it.

> I think it makes a great deal of difference whether or
> not the government funded R&D is done on force account or
> done by contract. If it is done on force account, then
> you are establishing a group of scientists who always will
> search for something to do.

> It is perfectly obvious now, for example, NASA is going
> to become an energy agency. It is going to become an energy
> agency simply because it exists. It no longer has a mission.
> And the House and Senate Space Committees want to give it
> a mission. And therefore, you are getting bills through
> Congress to put them in solar power, put them in geothermal
> power, to put them everywhere.

> A government contract program, on the other hand, has
> only the standard sort of political pressure of the Lockheed
> type to keep it going, which may be almost as powerful.
> But I do think it makes some difference as to how you do it.

In the discussion, one participant cautioned against exaggerating
the seriousness of inflexibility. He noted that nearly every successful R&D program at some point and usually at several points can be

killed by an unfriendly review. Projects pass through stages when the problems appear very difficult. Consequently, a reasonable degree of continuity or inflexibility can be a virtue.

Government Expenditures on Energy R&D

Many conferees, as has been noted, agreed a danger does exist that the government will rely more than it should on energy R&D funding and less on alternative measures in dealing with energy problems due to biases in the public decision-making process. Despite this possibility, many participants felt strongly that two billion dollars a year in government funding for energy R&D over the next five years was not too much, contrary to Part I. Given the seriousness of our energy problems, the importance of energy to our standard of living and national well-being, and the small amount of money involved compared with the total government budget or GNP, some thought that even more could be wisely spent.

> Certainly I don't think anybody feels that the dollar
> impact of spending two or three billion dollars a year in
> just terms of the money itself is really a problem . . . .

> If you take the broad view . . . that the purpose of
> the R&D is to look at all these options of providing inex-
> pensive, abundant energy in the future that is environ-
> mentally clean, provides low cost to the consumer, and is
> socially desirable from the point of view of life style,
> one could easily argue that you need a lot more R&D than
> what we are talking about.

Others, however, expressed reservations about this position citing the opportunities that are foregone in other areas when resources are diverted to energy R&D.

> We simply do not have an infinite reservoir of
> engineers, scientists, laboratories, and so on, to do
> energy R&D work . . . . So I think we have to not only
> consider what kind of energy R&D we are going to do,
> but whether or not we want to divert people from other
> activities into energy R&D.

In the longer term, of course, the number of engineers, scientists, and laboratories can be increased, but even then fewer people and resources

are available than would otherwise be the case for other activities. So
energy R&D can be carried too far in the sense that the benefits lost
because other activities must be curtailed or dropped exceed the benefits gained
from increasing energy R&D.

A different, though related, question that the conference addressed
concerns the proposed rate of increase in government spending on energy
R&D. On this issue there was considerably more uneasiness. This, in
part, arose because in the short run the supply of technical people and
facilities cannot be appreciably increased. Thus, the curtailments of
other R&D programs--the opportunity costs just discussed--are likely to
be particularly severe over the next several years if the proposed
increases in energy R&D are carried out. Better researchers are likely
to be drawn out of research per se and into R&D administration--searching
for competent people, finding office space, ordering equipment, and
performing other administrative functions.

Construction capacity needed to build new petroleum refineries,
electric power plants, and other facilities could also be a bottleneck
if sizable amounts of energy R&D funds are allocated to the construction
of pilot plants for coal gasification, oil shale, breeder reactors, and
other new energy technologies. Some conferees were also worried that the
planned surge in R&D activity might affect future R&D options and perhaps
freeze us into certain lines of activity and programs before their
desirability can be properly assessed.

Suggestions for Further Research

Throughout the conference numerous suggestions were made for further
research needed to improve our ability to develop sound energy R&D policies. The recommended topics dealt with deficiencies or gaps in our
present knowledge about the energy sector in general, about energy R&D
in particular, about the alternatives to government funding of energy
R&D, and about the process or procedures involved in formulating energy
R&D policies.

Energy Sector

> Quite clearly, we are operating in great ignorance of
> how energy markets work. And without that fundamental
> knowledge, much of the discussion of how R&D decisions
> should be made is going to be made in ignorance. One of
> the major research projects to pour your money into is
> how energy markets really work.

Many participants, like the one just quoted, felt that before we
could hope to develop rational energy R&D policies, we needed to know
much more about how the energy sector functions. How are prices set,
investment decisions made, and other aspects of firm conduct determined?
What government regulations most affect market behavior, and how? What
factors determine the amount and nature of R&D activity supported by
firms? How has new technology affected costs, competition, market
structure, and dependence on types of fuels and imports? Several
conferees recommended a historical study—or even a series of case
studies—of energy R&D over the last ten or twenty years, as one possible way to gain a better understanding of how R&D has interacted

with the complex mosaic of institutional features which varies so greatly from one energy industry to another.

Another important area that many felt deserves more attention involves identifying critical energy problems over the long run. As already noted, many participants expressed great concern during the conference about the adequacy of our energy resources for the period ten to fifty years in the future. Others had a different view of the resource picture and of the potential of prices and technology to alleviate possible shortages. They were much less concerned. Which of these two schools is correct has important implications for the scope and direction of energy R&D. If resources are inadequate, much more of our R&D effort needs to be directed toward new sources of energy supplies. And as was stressed during the conference, there may be other long-run problems that need R&D attention, such as increasing the security of energy supplies and reducing the environmental costs of energy production and use.

Another set of questions needing more research deals with the relationship between energy and societal welfare. Can the historical growth in energy consumption be slowed or stopped without reducing our standard of living? Can social science research modify societal values and goals regarding energy use? Can our transportation systems and living habits be altered to reduce energy needs without great hardship or inconvenience?

Energy R&D

Turning to energy R&D per se, we need to know more about what motivates firms supporting energy R&D and the individuals carrying out that research. For example, Part I suggests that changes in patent

policy probably would not significantly alter the incentives to conduct

energy R&D, but not all conferees agreed. As one participant pointed

out after the conference, the influence of patents is at a minimum

considerably more complicated than indicated in Part I.

> Probably one of the worst problems is the government's
> treatment of "background patents," i.e., patents developed
> with exclusively private funding, but used as the basis or
> starting point for the development of new technology (and
> patents) under government funding. The government usually
> claims title to these background patents in addition to
> the patents developed with its funding. In other words
> it operates on the principle that anything remotely touched
> by government funding, even indirectly, belongs to the
> government. The DOD policy has been of limited value
> because most DOD funding goes to large firms which are
> encouraged to set up separate divisions for their govern-
> ment business, as insulated as possible from their
> civilian business. DOD and NASA funding results in only
> about 10% as many patents per dollar of R&D expenditure
> as private funding.

Similarly we have only a rudimentary understanding of the ways that anti-

trust policy affects R&D incentives.

During the conference, many individuals expressed the belief that the

closer the R&D activity is to the ultimate user, the more likely it is to

produce results and the more likely the results will actually be trans-

ferred from the laboratory into the production process. Others, however,

argued that ultimately the efficacy of R&D depends on people, and good

people can be found in government laboratories, private research concerns,

and industry. This suggests that we need to know more about how the

research environment differs from one type of R&D facility to another,

and how differences affect the ability of facilities to attract good

researchers and in other ways influence the productivity of R&D. Similarly,

more information on the advantages and disadvantages of joint ventures

between the government and industry would be valuable. It would also
be helpful to know if, as some have suggested, a certain threshold level
of effort is necessary before energy R&D begins to be worthwhile. And
if so, what is the level and how does it vary from one energy field to
another?

Another aspect of energy R&D needing more study concerns the length
of time required for such R&D to produce useful results and for the results
to be deployed. As pointed out earlier, considerable disagreement exists
over this point. If energy R&D can have an important impact in the short
run, contrary to Part I, this alters the potential objectives and projects
for energy R&D.

More research was also recommended on the problems associated with
building up and cutting back energy R&D. Here historical studies of R&D
in space and other fields that have experienced a surge of public funds
followed by reduced support might be useful. A clearer understanding
would also be helpful of the critical energy R&D inputs--in what other
areas are they used, how is their demand in these areas likely to change,
how elastic is their supply in the short and long run, what substitutes
are available, how is the quality of R&D affected by shortages and use
of inferior inputs? And at the other end of the cycle, we need to know
how easily technical people and facilities can be moved out of energy R&D,
and what are the psychological and economic costs of such shifts.

Alternatives to Energy R&D Funding

Part I argues that public policy in determining how much to fund
energy R&D should consider all possible alternatives to such funding.

By way of illustration, it discusses a few possible alternatives, but a much more comprehensive and thorough examination of the alternatives is necessary. This should include not only a comprehensive list of the alternatives but also some indication of their relative advantages and disadvantages compared to energy R&D funding and each other. Moreover, for any particular alternative, such as tax incentives, numerous variants may need to be considered.

Formulating Energy R&D Policy

The conferees, as has been noted, were quite divided on the usefulness of benefit-cost analysis in determining the amount and distribution of resources the government should allocate to energy R&D. This suggests that more work is needed to identify to what extent and in what ways benefit-cost analysis can be useful.

We could also use more information about the political process by which energy R&D policy is forged. How does the public's conception of energy problems affect that policy? What factors determine how the public perceives energy problems and the role of R&D in solving these problems? How can public opinion be guided to conform more closely to the realities of the energy situation and the role that R&D can perform? To what extent can public attitudes reduce the potential effectiveness of energy R&D policy? How clear are the signals generated by the political process regarding the goals and priorities for energy R&D? Can decision makers get useful guidance from the political system? If so, how?

These are all issues raised at the conference and considered worthy of further research. Indeed, in some cases, participants felt that more research was essential before we could hope to improve the formulation of energy R&D policy.

APPENDICES

Appendix I

OTHER REASONS FOR GOVERNMENT INTERVENTION

A number of other reasons, besides those described in Chapter 3, are frequently cited to justify greater government funding of energy R&D. These reasons are identified in this appendix and their validity or importance questioned.

1. _Availability of funds_. A good example of this argument is provided by the following quote from a 1972 Presidential message on science and technology:[1]

> I believe it is appropriate for the Federal Government to encourage private research and development to the extent that the market mechanism is not effective in bringing needed innovations into use. This can happen in a number of circumstances. For example, the sheer size of some development projects is beyond the reach of private firms, particularly in industries which are fragmented into many small companies . . . .

As the President's statement suggests, there are two variants to the availability-of-funds argument. The first maintains that in some industries firms are so numerous and small that they simply do not have the resources required to conduct a sufficient amount of R&D. The coal industry is frequently cited as an example. By itself, however, this is not a sufficient justification for government support, for small firms with profitable R&D opportunities can often raise the requisite capital either by borrowing or issuing new equity. While some may argue that imperfections in the capital market prevent this, the experiences of American firms in research intensive fields, such as the semiconductor industry, would question this

---

[1] This message was delivered on March 16, 1972, and is cited in _Task Force Report on Energy R&D_, p. 155.

contention. Moreover, even if for the sake of argument one assumes that the capital market functions poorly, government support may still not be necessary. If larger firms outside the industry are aware of the promising R&D opportunities and can hire the expertise needed to exploit them, they should have an incentive to move into the industry and carry out the desired R&D. The entry of many large petroleum firms into the coal industry over the last generation and the conglomerate merger movement in general would support this possibility.

The second variant of the availability-of-funds argument contends that some R&D projects are too expensive for any private firm regardless of size to support. The breeder reactor program is typically used as an illustration. The market fails in this situation not because social costs and benefits differ from private costs and benefits, but because the huge capital requirements pose an absolute barrier preventing private enterprise from carrying out the project even though the net private benefits are positive.

There are, however, several reasons for believing that projects of such magnitude are relatively rare. First, the internal resources of the larger American corporations are substantial, as the billions of dollars that IBM poured into the development of its 360 series of computer illustrates.[1] Second, nearly all of the large and well-known corporations can raise considerable sums of money through debt and equity financing. Third, firms can form consortia for undertaking large projects. This has become an increasingly popular method of financing large foreign mineral developments

---

[1] T. A. Wise, "IBM's $5,000,000,000 Gamble," Fortune (September 1966), pp. 118-23+. Also see "IBM's $3.8-Billion Cookie Jar," Business Week (February 2, 1974), p. 22.

in recent years. EPRI is another example of a cooperative effort. Fourth, although the expensive and spectacular R&D projects often receive the most publicity, the majority of projects are not inordinately costly. Indeed, research on R&D costs in general indicates that most projects are not beyond the means of medium sized firms as the following quote from a well-known industrial organization text suggests:[1]

> A more fruitful way of considering the technical opportunities confronting small and large firms is to visualize a frequency distribution of development projects, ordered according to their cost. A census would undoubtedly reveal the distribution to be highly skewed. The spectacularly costly projects which receive the most attention in newspapers and trade journals are few in number, forming the distribution's long thin tail. Smaller projects are much more numerous, giving rise to a peak or mode in a spending range somewhere between $50,000 and $300,000. The parameters of this distribution have been shifting over time; that is, the model R&D project today is more expensive than its counterpart 30 years ago. But firm sizes have also been rising secularly . . . .

Even if the typical R&D project in the energy field were two or three times more expensive than the average for all R&D projects, the capital requirements for the vast majority of energy projects would still lie within the capabilities of the private sector.

2. <u>Risk pooling and discounting</u>. Another argument frequently encountered in the energy R&D literature maintains that government support for high risk projects is essential if these projects are to receive adequate funding. Again, two major lines of reasoning can be identified. The first points out that many more R&D projects are undertaken within a large country such as the United States than in any single firm, and so large countries can benefit more from the pooling of risks. This means that a high risk project increases the overall risk associated with a

---

[1]Scherer, p. 355.

126

country's R&D program less than the overall risk associated with the R&D
program of a firm considering the project. The latter will, consequently,
tend to discount the project more for risk than is appropriate from
society's viewpoint.

Conceivably, a private insurance program could reduce the risk for
firms. But no such insurance now exists, and given the adverse effects
insurance would likely have on the incentives of firms conducting R&D, it
probably will not become available. Thus, public support for high risk
projects would appear desirable. Such support, however, is justified only
for projects that are both costly and risky since the opportunities within firms for pooling risks associated with smaller projects are generally
sufficient. This suggests that the number of high risk projects qualifying
for public support is not very large because the more risky projects are
concentrated at the basic research end of the R&D spectrum and the more
expensive projects at the development end.[1]

The second line of reasoning supporting government funding for high
risk projects postulates that the discount rate for risk is higher for most
firms than for society. As a result, private enterprise discriminates
against high risk projects more than optimal. Whether firms on average
actually have higher discount rates for risk than society as a whole,
however, is uncertain. Indeed, it is not entirely clear why they should.

3. _Time discounting and the welfare of future generations_. A similar
argument contends that most firms have higher discount rates for time[2] than

---

[1] For some interesting empirical evidence on differences in the technical
risks between research projects and development projects based on a sample
of 20 chemical and petroleum firms, see Edwin Mansfield, et al., Chap. 2.

[2] Chapter 3 pointed out that nearly everyone would rather have a dollar of
additional income today than later. The intensity of this preference is
reflected in an individual's discount rate for time by which he discounts
or depreciates future income in comparison with present income.

society. As a result, government support for projects with long gesta-

tion and payoff periods is necessary. The validity of this proposition is

not easy to appraise. On one hand, there is evidence that most of the

projects carried out by firms are short term. For example, a McGraw-Hill

survey in the early sixties found that the manufacturing firms expected

89 percent of their R&D expenditures to pay off in five years or less.[1]

Even after making allowances for possible changes in the intervening

decade and for miscalculations on the part of firms, this is still a

surprisingly short period. Interestingly, though, firms in the petroleum

and coal industry, the one industry identified that was clearly in the

energy sector, indicated that they expected only 50 percent of their R&D

expenditures to pay off within five years. Moreover, even if one concludes

that firms have high time discount rates, the a priori reasons for believing

the social discount rate is different do not all suggest that the latter

will be lower. Corporation managers and their stockholders are older than

the population in general, and this may contribute to a higher discount

rate for firms. But these individuals also are richer than the general

population which should have the opposite effect.

Differences in preferences between the rich and the poor raise an

interesting question regarding the appropriate means of determining the

---

[1]McGraw-Hill, Business Plans for Expenditures on Plant and Equipment (annual)
as cited in Edwin Mansfield, et al., p. 7.

Such short payoff periods suggest that R&D activity often produces results
in a relatively short time span. This may cause some to question the contention made in Chapter 4 that R&D is rarely an appropriate policy instrument
for achieving short-run objectives of energy policy. However, it is important to remember that most industrial R&D activity with quick payoff periods
produces marginal advances in technology, and such advances are not likely
to have a significant impact on the energy sector as a whole. In addition,
new innovations are likely to pay for their R&D costs long before they
appreciably affect the supply or demand for energy in the United States.

social discount rate for time (or for risk). In the marketplace, an individual has as many votes as he has dollars, but when it comes to public
elections (to which public officials are presumably more sensitive), he
has one vote like everyone else. Thus, should the social discount rate
merely be an average of the rate for all members of society or should each
member's preference be weighted by his command over economic resources?
Economists and others can speculate on such questions and clarify certain
issues, but ultimately the decision is a value judgment.

Along these lines, some individuals argue that society as a whole
should consider not only the preferences of its present members, but also
take into account the welfare of future generations. Again, this is
largely a value judgment which this analysis cannot resolve. However,
it can raise certain questions that need to be considered in the evaluation. Historically, the material standard of living has been improving
with time, at least in the industrially advanced nations. If this trend
continues, government programs that divert resources from present consumption to energy R&D will effect an intergeneration redistribution of
wealth that accentuates inequality. Is this what society wants? Second,
to the extent that the government is successful in depressing the time
rate of discount, this is likely to postpone or slow down the consumption
of energy resources and at the same time to stimulate energy R&D. One
possible consequence is that new energy sources will replace the present
ones long before the production costs of the latter rise to the point
where the sacrifices required of today's generation are justified. This
is particularly likely if the private market is better able than the
government to assess the effects of the depletion of energy resources
and the potential of new technology to offset these effects.

129

4. <u>Income distribution</u>. In allocating funds for energy R&D, firms are guided, at least in part, by the expected profits associated with various projects. These profits depend, among other things, on the need or demand they will satisfy if successfully completed. Since demand is a function of individual preferences plus the distribution of income, one can argue, if the distribution of income is not optimal, that the market signals firms receive do not accurately reflect the benefits to society. In which case, some government action is necessary to correct this distortion. For example, if low income individuals are more concerned than the population in general about the cost of distributing electric power and less concerned about distributing it underground, and if a more equitable distribution of income is deemed desirable, an optimal energy R&D policy would require that the government intervene to shift R&D incentives toward the former objective and away from the latter. Just how much weight should be attached to the income distribution argument for intervention in energy R&D is hard to say without making a value judgment as to how the present income distribution differs from the optimal. However, there are easier, more direct, and more efficient ways for the government to deal with inequities in income distribution.

5. <u>Employment of scientists and engineers</u>. About 1967 the phenomenal growth in R&D expenditures that the American economy had enjoyed since the early postwar years began to taper off. Yet universities, geared up to fulfill ever increasing demands for new scientists and engineers, had many students in their long education pipelines and continued to pump highly trained people into the market. This coupled with severe cutbacks in certain fields, particularly those relating to space

and defense activities, created an unemployment problem for scientists and engineers.

One argument for increasing government sponsored energy R&D is that it would put to good use these highly trained individuals. Since these individuals are unemployed, the opportunity cost to society of using them on energy R&D is much less than the private costs to the firms that hire them. Without questioning the validity of the latter point, most economists would caution against increasing public support for energy R&D solely for this reason. First and probably most serious, such a program while alleviating the temporary hardship of unemployment (even conceding that temporary may in some cases be the rest of a lifetime) removes the incentives for the next generation of students to look to other disciplines for a vocation and for those already trained to find new careers where their productivity to society would be greater. In addition, once a subsidy is started, as postwar agricultural policy illustrates, it tends to perpetuate itself by augmenting the vested interests most concerned that such support continues regardless of its inefficiencies. Thus, the ultimate social costs may far outweigh the temporary social benefits. The desirability of such programs must also be questioned because increasing energy R&D may not appreciably lighten the unemployment of scientists and engineers with skills and expertise specific to space and defense applications.

6. _Competition._ Some have argued that the government should support energy R&D to strengthen competition in this sector of the economy. The reasoning behind this argument is seldom spelled out. If the point is merely that public R&D funds decrease the distortion caused by the

nonappropriability of some R&D benefits and thereby reduce the need for
anti-competitive patent laws and more lax anti-trust regulations, the argument is just a variant of those discussed in Chapter 3.

Another possible interpretation of this argument is that the government should try to influence the direction of technological change in such
a manner that competition is stimulated. This implies that public policy
should try to foster new sources of energy to compete with present sources
and to divert R&D away from technologies that increase capital requirements and economies of scale toward technologies with the opposite characteristics. Such efforts, however, seem misdirected for energy R&D. Much
of this sector of the economy is regulated, and in the regulated industries
little attempt is made to rely on competition to effect good industry performance. In addition, directing R&D away from the most promising projects
reduces its efficiency. And finally, predicting _ex ante_ the competitive
implications of new technology is extremely hazardous. For example, one
might have concluded in the early fifties that the basic oxygen process
would reduce competition in the American steel industry since it increased
economies of scale. However, it used considerably less scrap than the open
hearth process that it replaced. This depressed the price of scrap, and
stimulated the rise of the electric furnace and the mini-mill. In addition,
the basic oxygen process apparently improved the competitive position of
foreign producers, particularly the Japanese, in the American market. Thus,
the overall consequences of the basic oxygen process for competition are
far from clear even today, more than twenty years after a decision on the
competitive implications of the process would have to have been made.

7. <u>Government purchases</u>. One encounters occasionally the argument
that the government must be prepared to fund the R&D required to develop
the new products and processes that the government itself needs, such as
a new fuel for a rocket or a new fuel cell for a submarine. By itself,
however, this is not a valid argument. For if the government is willing
to pay a price for the goods and services it needs that covers the expected costs of development as well as production, private firms have an
incentive to fund the necessary R&D. It is true that this incentive will
be diluted and perhaps inadequate if the potential results of the R&D are
of interest only to the government, since once the desired technology is
achieved the firm is at the mercy of a single buyer who may choose to
exercise its monopsonistic power. However, the greater the potential
application of the R&D for civilian needs, the smaller the required R&D
effort, and the greater the expected profitability of government purchases,
the less likely firms will be deterred. The latter factor suggests that
the government may have to pay more for its R&D if it leaves the funding
and risk with the private sector. But countering this tendency is the
likely possibility that such an arrangement will increase the incentives
of firms to conduct the necessary R&D efficiently and to bring it to early
fruition.

Appendix II

PARTICIPANTS TO THE RFF CONFERENCE ON
"PUBLIC POLICY AND ENERGY R&D," APRIL 18-19, 1974
(with major affiliation at time of conference)

John Andelin
Representative McCormack's Office

Peter Auer
Cornell University

Davis Bobrow
University of Minnesota

David B. Brooks
Canadian Department of Energy,
    Mines and Resources

Harvey Brooks
Harvard University

Irwin C. Bupp
Harvard University

Paul P. Craig
National Science Foundation

Joel Darmstadter
Resources for the Future

W. Kenneth Davis
Bechtel Power Corporation

Jean-Claude Derian
Massachusetts Institute of Technology

John H. DeYoung, Jr.
Pennsylvania State University

Warren H. Donnelly
Library of Congress

John Ferejohn
California Institute of Technology

Leonard L. Fischman
Resources for the Future

Samuel Globe
Battelle Memorial Institute

Bruce Hannay
Bell Laboratories

J. Herbert Hollomon
Massachusetts Institute of Technology

F. Holloway
EXXON Corporation

Hans H. Landsberg
Resources for the Future

Joseph Lerner
Federal Energy Office

Henry R. Linden
Institute of Gas Technology

H. G. MacPherson
Institute for Energy Analysis

William McCormick
Office of Management and Budget

Stephen L. McDonald
University of Texas

Laurence Moss
National Academy of Engineering

Richard R. Nelson
Yale University

John F. O'Leary
Atomic Energy Commission

Philip Palmedo
Federal Energy Office

Harry Perry
Resources for the Future

John H. Schanz, Jr.
University of Denver

Sam H. Schurr
Electric Power Research Institute

Mark Sharefkin
Resources for the Future

E. Keith Thomson
Bechtel Power Corporation

John E. Tilton
Pennsylvania State University

William A. Vogely
Department of the Interior

Alvin M. Weinberg
Federal Energy Office

Frederick J. Wells
Resources for the Future

Charles Zraket
MITRE Corporation